FALL INJURY PREVENTION FOR OLDER ADULTS ...

FALL INJURY PREVENTION FOR OLDER ADULTS ...

And Those Who Care About Them

Joanne M. Price,
Fall Prevention Educator
Contributions By: Brett Longo, PT,
Patricia-Jo Dean, RN,
and Amy McAllister, Registered Dietitian

iUniverse, Inc.
New York Lincoln Shanghai

Fall Injury Prevention for Older Adults …
And Those Who Care About Them

iUniverse books may be ordered through booksellers or by contacting:

iUniverse
2021 Pine Lake Road, Suite 100
Lincoln, NE 68512
www.iuniverse.com
1-800-Authors (1-800-288-4677)

The views expressed in this work are solely those of the author and do not necessarily reflect the views of the publisher, and the publisher hereby disclaims any responsibility for them.

All information, suggestions, advice, tips and programs presented in this book are informational only. Review the information and recommendations in this book with your healthcare provider prior to implementation. Although written to be as comprehensive as possible, this book is not meant to be all-inclusive and is for educational purposes only. The authors and contributors of this book disclaim any responsibility for injuries resulting from performing or practicing any of the information, suggestions, advice, tips and programs presented in this book.

ISBN-13: 978-0-595-42016-2 (pbk)
ISBN-13: 978-0-595-86359-4 (ebk)
ISBN-10: 0-595-42016-8 (pbk)
ISBN-10: 0-595-86359-0 (ebk)

Printed in the United States of America

Injuries resulting from accidental falls are a growing and often devastating problem for older adults. Whether for yourself, a partner, parent, or friend, this guide will help you understand the causes of falls, and provide easy to implement tips for reducing the risk of falls and fall related injuries. Through the use of the recommendations in this book, it is easy to increase the safety and well-being of yourself and those you care about.

Author: Joanne Price, CEO, Integricare Corporation
& Fall Prevention Educator
Contributors: Patricia-Jo Dean, Registered Nurse
Amy McAllister, Registered Dietitian
Brett Longo, Licensed Physical Therapist

Contents

Acknowledgements

Thank you to everyone who contributed or provided support during the writing of this book. In addition, thank you to all who lent their encouragement to this project. Special thanks to my co-authors, reviewers, and contributors, whose expertise in the field of healthcare for older adults has assured comprehensive coverage of the topic.

Thank you to my extraordinarily patient and loving husband, Marc, and beloved children Sarah and Ryan, without whom I would not have the courage to pursue my dreams. Thank you to my parents, siblings and extended family for your support and encouragement.

Lastly, to all the older adults who inspired me to write this book through their encouraging and motivating stories of perseverance in difficult circumstances, you are all heroes in my book. Thank you.

Foreword

By: Joanne Price

My life's work got a late start. I didn't know "what I wanted to be when I grew up" until I was 40 years old. My personal path was triggered by a family event, which moved me so much that I felt compelled to change the direction of my life. The story goes like this:

While being the primary caregiver for my ailing father, my beloved stepmother had neglected her own health (a very common scenario). A few months after his passing, she began to pay attention to her own health and discovered some significant problems. The situation culminated in her needing double bypass heart surgery. During her recovery from the surgery, we were having a phone conversation and she mentioned that her physician was strongly recommending she begin a regular exercise program as part of her successful rehabilitation. Being both unfamiliar with organized exercise programs and not considering herself 'that kind of person', she was reluctant to take the one exercise class that was offered in her senior community.

This conversation spurred me to do some research on the topic of senior exercise. I was struck by the lack of quality exercise programs made available to seniors, so I decided to become a senior exercise specialist myself. I had some dance experience and certainly spent enough time in the gym to be able to work out a solid program that would be both enjoyable and beneficial to older adults. I worked with an accreditation company, American Fitness Professionals and Associates (AFPA), and became certified in several exercise disciplines focused on older adults. I then volunteered at the local YMCA to 'hone my skills'. Before I knew it, being 40 and entering the fitness field didn't seem so daunting. It became apparent that my age was actually an advantage when working in the area of 'older adult' fitness, so my journey began.

Standing in front of my first class, after hundreds of hours of practice, the music began. I think a version of 'Fly me to the Moon' was the warm up song—and away we all went. Working with older adults provided me a level of personal and professional satisfaction that I had not experienced previously. Always wanting to reach more people, I applied for and was granted funds from a local public access TV channel to produce an exercise program for those who did not want, or were unable, to attend an exercise class. The program, called *Stairway to Fitness* aired for over two years in San Diego. I remain very proud of the contribution this show made in the wellbeing of many people who faithfully 'worked out' with that program.

Teaching exercise and personal training with older adults was very rewarding and I did that for several years. However, I needed to do more to help my beloved population. So, I purchased a franchise and opened a homecare agency. We provided non-medical in home care for older and disabled adults. Boy, was that an eye opener. I was now working for families and seniors who only wished they could go to an exercise class! Most of my clients were frail and, in many cases, were experiencing the advanced stages of severe and debilitating chronic conditions such as Alzheimer's, Osteoporosis, and Parkinson's disease.

Home care is a 24/7 job for agency owners, especially for those who really care about their clients. It is also expensive, as worker's compensation (in California, anyway) adds about 20% to the cost of an employees wages, which is obviously transferred to the clients price of care. It is common to pay between $18 and $22 per hour or more for in home care. I could not help many of the people who called my agency, due to their financial constraints. Also, many older adults did not want a stranger in their home and would not accept in home care.

At this point, I felt I needed to do even more—so I bought yet another company. Good thing my husband and I had home equity to borrow against, as my philanthropic side many times outweighs the available funds in my pocketbook! We bought a medical alarm distributorship for the county we live in called ResponseLink (national company, local authorized distributorships). We now provide affordable, on call, help to seniors. This enables me to provide 24/7 peace of mind to our subscribers and their families. With the press of a waterproof, pendant based button, help is on the line (two-way voice communication included) to call for appropriate assistance for the subscriber for any emergency, medical or otherwise.

So there I was, helping older adults and feeling pretty darn good about it. Except, now there seemed to be no time to teach exercise anymore. Working what seemed like around the clock, yet missing that daily interaction with 'my older adults', I needed to find an outlet. Enter Fall Prevention! The county Aging and Independence Services was seeking a volunteer to head its 'Fall Prevention Task Force' to provide outreach and education to the community on Fall Injury Prevention. I scooped up the opportunity, as it is obviously related to my business, it would be a good networking fit for my company and get me back out with 'my people' by teaching fall prevention techniques.

Over the past few years, I have immersed myself in fall prevention information and provided over 90 fall prevention workshops to senior groups and caregiver support groups. My experience in homecare, exercise and home safety have all come together to help me create a comprehensive program. During this time, I felt that the information in my presentations needed to be brought to the sons, daughters, neighbors and healthcare providers of those at risk. Hence, this book—*Fall Prevention for Older Adults and Those Who Care About Them*.

The advice contained herein is a guide, use what you need and leave the rest. Everybody is dealing with a different set of circumstances. Share this book with anyone who needs it. Working together, we may prevent tragedies from occurring due to falls; including, loss of independence, broken hips, hospitalization, and premature death. About 30% of falls are preventable!

You may be among that 30% if you follow the advice in this book. Use it as a workbook, remembering to consult with your healthcare provider before tackling any of the exercises or implementing any of the recommendations. Some of the advice is best carried out with the help of someone who can help clear the clutter, move the cookware, install grab bars, etc.

Not being an expert in all things (even though my husband may say I think otherwise), I have recruited expert help in the writing of this book. Brett Longo, a Physical Therapist, contributed information relating to the components of balance. He also includes appropriate exercises and stretches to increase and maintain balance, thereby lessening fall risk. Patricia-Jo Dean is a Registered Nurse and has worked in the health care field for over 35 years. She contributed medication related information and advice. Amy McAllister, Registered Dietitian, who has been working with seniors for over 15 year's, reviewed the information on the importance of proper nutrition and hydration for reducing fall risk and yours truly—Joanne Price, pulling it all together, adding anecdotes, and writing on home safety.

It is the collective goal of all who have contributed to this project that this book is helpful to you and those you care for in prolonging an independent and healthy lifestyle. Remember, the only difference between knowing and doing is motivation. Let's do it!

As Jackie Gleason used to say, "And away we go!"

Introduction

Although everyone is at some degree of risk from falls, fall injuries in the senior population (ages 64 and above) are much higher. For many, fall risk increases with each passing year. Falls can be a result of a single accidental 'slip' or may have multiple causes. Risk factors often combine to present an extremely high risk of falling and significant injury. We call this a 'layering' of risk factors. Some of us have one risk factor, small or significant. Others may have several risk factors in their daily lives, presenting a layered risk. Whether you have one or several risk factors in your life, this book can help.

As falls are the leading cause of emergency room visits and accidental death in the senior population, lowering the number of falls and fall related injuries could have a positive and significant effect on the already strained healthcare system. Whether you are a senior citizen, a family member, healthcare provider, loved one, friend, caregiver or neighbor, you can contribute in a multitude of ways to the increased safety, through using the information presented in this guide and the sample forms provided for risk assessment and home safety.

This guide covers the following subjects as they relate to falls and fall related injuries for the senior population of 65 and over and those on multiple medications who are dealing with chronic, often debilitating diseases. You will learn:

- Statistics related to falls
- Risk factors related to falls
- Habitat Factors/Home Safety
- Role of Chronic Disease
- Medication Related Factors
- Hydration and Nutritional Factors
- Balance/Posture Factors
- Exercise and the Role of Muscle Atrophy

- Walking Assistance Equipment Usage
- Strategy on how to fall and get up safely from a fall if possible.

Also included are forms to use, including a home safety checklist, and a medication evaluation form. **Recommendations** are labeled and are highlighted in each section.

I've met many older adults that were vibrant, healthy and optimistic, some in their 80's and 90's who, after a fall, became despondent and literally gave up on life and thoughts of going home again and living independently. Unfortunately, this story is lived over and over again by thousands of fall victims. Rehabilitation from a fall, especially a broken hip or head trauma, takes an immense amount of will power and with many people, having little or no family to help motivate them, painfully and quietly wither away. If we learn how to reduce the risk of falling—lives may be saved, maybe even your own.

Statistics

Statistics indicate that between 30-40% of people over 65 fall each year. Unfortunately, after an initial fall, the odds of falling just about double! Many studies track emergency room visits for their statistics. Since a many falls go unrecorded, the percentage of falls is probably higher than reported. Women are three times more likely than men to be hospitalized for fall related injuries. Older adult men are 22% more likely than women to die as a result of a fall. Some falls are due to risky behaviors (climbing on ladders, drinking alcohol while on multiple medications, etc), while others are due to environment (clutter) or physical weakness.

Frail adults, those with impaired strength, mobility, balance, and endurance—are twice as likely to fall as healthier persons of the same age, and they sustain more severe injuries when they fall. Of those who fall, 20% to 30% suffer moderate to severe injuries such as hip fractures or head traumas that reduce mobility, independence and increase the risk of premature death.

Although, many people that fall are not injured significantly enough to warrant a visit to the emergency room, it takes much longer to heal from cuts, bumps and bruises the older we get and these types of falls may have ongoing negative effects on a person's physiology. Falls often also result in an increased of fear of falling again. For those that fall and are injured it is not unusual to for them to be hospitalized for days, weeks or even months. Hospitalization rates for hip fractures are highest among Caucasian women. This difference may be due, in part, to the higher prevalence of osteoporosis among Caucasian females.

Hospitalization and the resulting stay at a skilled nursing facility (aka; SNF) can cause a spiraling downward of a patients physical and psychological well-being. Victims of fall related fractures are five times more likely to move into a nursing or residential institution within 24 months of a fall. For those of advanced age, patients may become depressed and feel that they will not recover. Two thirds of all senior citizens who fall will experience a repeat fall within six months of the original incident.

In the numerous fall prevention workshops I have presented, many participants have informed me that costs of falls that they have experienced came, with a very hefty price tag. One woman announced that her broken hip and subsequent long road to wellness cost $60,000! This, of course, does not include ongoing costs of medication, home health requirements or long-term care.

The cost of modifications in ones home, which can significantly lower fall risk, can cost under $300. Moreover, home modifications can be made one at a time, so as not to seem overwhelming. I'm a big list maker. Lists help me focus and prioritize. Making a list may be helpful to you as well. You have a list, you complete one of the items on the list, cross it off, and move on to the next item. Little by little, you will accomplish your objective. Enlisting the assistance of loved ones or hiring help can accomplish your goal quickly of living in a safer environment.

The highest cost one can pay for a fall is the cost of lost independence. Whether you are a senior, the son or daughter of an older adult, or a person who works with or cares about a senior, we can all relate to that cost as being the highest cost one can pay.

Like anything else, you can pay a little or a lot for home modifications and professional physical therapy or exercise instruction, that depends on your personal choice and situation. We present solutions in this guide that take no money at all and some that do cost time and money. In the long run, the benefits far outweigh the cost. You have the power to direct your destiny in lowering your risk of falling—this book will help you take control—you can do it!

Causes of Increased Fall Risk among Older Adults

As we age, our bodies and minds undergo changes that may cause either a gradual or a rapid decline in bodily functions and mental capacity. For some, the physical aspect of living with chronic pain or a chronic disease that becomes difficult. For others, the mental or emotional aspect is the most challenging. The rate of individual decline is partly genetic, partly environmental and partly the lifestyle choices made over a long period.

For some, fall risk increase is due to the use of multiple medications. For others, fall risk is increased due to failing eyesight and balance, while someone else's fall risk may be increased due to neuropathy or muscle weakness. Fall risk can be grouped into two categories, intrinsic (internal) and extrinsic (external) causes. Depending on the root cause(s) for the increased risk, you can develop a plan that may counter that increase, helping you feel more safe and confident. Risk factors are detailed throughout the book, as are recommended ways to lower your personal fall risk.

INTRINSIC (INTERNAL) CAUSES INCLUDE:

- Chronic Disease
- Medication Side-Effects
- Conditions of the Eyes and Ears
- Balance Problems
- Improper Posture
- Foot Conditions
- Lack of Muscle Mass

- Fear of Falling
- General Physical Decline
- Mental Decline
- Loss of Bone Mass
- Poor Vision

Chronic Disease in Fall Risk

As we age, any number of chronic diseases can take hold. Although chronic and degenerative disease can strike at any age, arthritis, diabetes, high blood pressure, lupus, multiple sclerosis, osteoporosis, and heart disease are usually conditions associated with onset in our elder years. Symptoms from chronic conditions may differ, but the effects of the symptoms may be the same. For example, pain, whether from headache, backache or nerve pain may cause distraction and depression, both of which increase fall risk.

Neuropathy in the lower extremities, caused by diabetes or other condition can increase fall risk due to pain, numbness or being unable to 'feel' your feet on the floor. Falls are a common problem for people with certain degenerative diseases, including advanced diabetes, Parkinson's disease and multiple sclerosis, ALS, post-polio syndrome and many other diseases.

As you may know, if symptoms of the disease doesn't cause falls, the medications one needs to take to help control the disease or it's symptoms may contribute to the likelihood of a fall occurring. Being aware of any symptoms that might develop in any chronic conditions and, side effects of medications you may take to help alleviate symptoms, gives you the power to be pro-active in adjusting home or lifestyle to lower the risk of fall related injuries.

For example, if you know that your medication may cause drowsiness, do not ignore the warning. If you become drowsy every time you take a particular medication, it would be prudent to make sure your home was as safe as possible. Each section of this book examines a specific contributor to increases in fall risk and provides recommendations on lowering your fall risk in that category. The end of the book covers exercise programming and 'how to fall correctly'. Whether medication related, physiological, or environmental, we have included valuable, practical and easy to implement information for you here in this guide.

EXTRINSIC (EXTERNAL) CAUSES INCLUDE:

- Indoor Hazards
- Outdoor Hazards
- Mobility Aids
- Distraction (noise or thoughts)
- Loose Clothing
- Inadequate Footwear
- Progressive Lenses

Three W's of Falls Awareness

Awareness of the reason(s) why, where and when falls occur both inside and outside the home can provide valuable information in the prevention of future falls. You are encouraged to practice the 3W's of falls awareness. Fall risk may be decreased by tracking the 3W's of falls. Use of the 3W's may help decrease risk of serious injury through awareness of the when, where and why of your particular situation.

Let's begin with **WHEN**. The timing of a fall or loss of balance may yield helpful important information in preventing a future fall. If an individual fell at 10am and took meds at 9am (or didn't take the medications at the proper times), he may be able to decrease fall risk simply by using a medication reminder or log or speaking to his healthcare provider about changing the time of day of dosage. Have medications re-evaluated by a doctor or pharmacist to check for contraindications or hazards. Did the fall happen at night? Could bedding or loose fitting night cloths be the culprit?

> **RECOMMENDATION:** Record the time of day and circumstances of your fall accident. See Appendix for a sample form.

WHERE did the fall occur? Many household falls occur in the bathroom. This room is both a friend and a foe. Protect yourself with installation of some safety equipment including weight bearing bars (grab bars) to aid shower entrance and exit. Elimination of clutter and a heightened commode seat for easier 'on and off' the toilet are helpful as well.

Write down the circumstances of a fall, including the time of day and location to learn **WHY** the fall happened. This will also provide valuable information for your physician or care provider who can help eliminate the hazard or lessen the chances of falling again. A leading cause of death for people over 65 is fall related injuries or conditions brought on by falls. Be proactive to remain independent.

Rushing to the bathroom is hazardous, as is being distracted. Give yourself enough time, if possible, to get where you need to go without rushing. Falling on the way to the bathroom can be due to not allowing enough time for your body to adjust to standing after lying prone for a number of hours.

> **RECOMMENDATION:** Give your self a few moments standing, wiggle your toes and loosen your hips to increase circulation and equilibrium before proceeding to the bathroom.

Certain behaviors that may have seemed safe in the past, could represent a fall risk due to muscular atrophy, chronic conditions or medications. For example, be extra careful when tilting your head back under a showerhead and closing your eyes at the same time to rinse products from your hair. Closing your eyes and tilting your head back may cause you to lose your balance. This is a behavior that many of us have done on an almost daily basis for a great number years when showering. Unfortunately, this action could be devastating if performed at an increased age, especially if you are taking a number of medications.

> **RECOMMENDATION:** Install a removable showerhead on a cord, so you do not have to tilt your head back to rinse. Better yet, sit down on a shower seat and hold the showerhead to rinse your hair.

For some older adults taking blood pressure medication, the act of bending over, in the shower to pick up a dropped washcloth, for example, can cause blood pressure to drop so rapidly that they become dizzy, disoriented or even lose consciousness. Don't be afraid, but do be aware and, modify your home and behaviors accordingly.

Balance

Author: Brett Longo, P.T.
Contributions by: Joanne Price

In this section, we look at how your body's loss of function can contribute to falls. The body's balance system can be broken down into six interacting components. Each of the six components can be compromised with age. As we grow older, our body slows, making it difficult for the six components to communicate with each other as rapidly as in the past, this decrease in communication between systems creates opportunities for falls to occur.

In order for the balance system to function properly, three things must occur. First, the system has to collect information. Information is received from receptors in your feet, eyes, and inner ear. The information allows your brain to know where your limbs are in relation to your head and where your head is in relation to your body.

Your brain collects all this information, and quickly decides what your body needs to do in order for you to stay balanced. Often, with age, this information gathering, decision making and response slows, because our nerves conduct the signal slower. This is one reason why the demands to stay up on our feet become more difficult as we age.

This section concludes by demonstrating specific exercises to do at home that will help you increase and maintain your balance. Your balance is like a muscle, if you exercise it, it will get stronger. The exercises outlined in this book are unique for increasing your balance. They are specific to training your balance system, you can do them as often as you want and there is no need to worry about over exercising. In fact, the more often you do these exercises, the faster your balance will improve.

NOTE: As with all exercise and advice found in this book, check with your healthcare provider before attempting. Not all exercises are right for every person. It is important to know your own limits and work within them to strengthen your body.

THE SIX COMPONENTS OF YOUR BALANCE SYSTEM

Vision

While attending physical therapy school, a group of students conducted a study on balance. They had young college age athletes walk on a treadmill for an extended period of time as they filmed them. What they were trying to determine was how vision was used to aid in balance control. The subjects wore a hood over their head and then asked to walk on the treadmill again. All of them, as athletic as they were, fell off the treadmill. This study demonstrated the importance of vision to the balance system. This study, and many like it, proves that vision is the most domineering component of the balance system.

As we age, our vision tends to worsen. As for myself, just entering into my forties, I am not quite able to see street signs as clearly as I used to. It is common to see individuals as they enter their forties needing to wear glasses to read or drive. As we venture into later stages of life, not only do we have problems with visual acuity, but we also run into diseases that affect our vision as well. Conditions including cataracts, glaucoma, and macular degeneration, as well as normal decrease in visual acuity play a role in our decreased ability to balance.

As mentioned at the beginning of this chapter, the balance system needs to collect information, process it and send out the proper and necessary response to that information. If we cannot clearly see, where we are placing our feet or see certain hazards due to poor lighting, the chance for falling increases significantly. Unfortunately, as we grow older, one fall is all it takes for us to risk losing our independence. See the chapter on home safety in this book for suggestions on increasing the lighting in your surroundings to help lessen your fall risk.

Precaution: Pay special attention to your surroundings if you wear *progressive lens eyewear*. If you look down towards a curb for instance, you may be looking through the bifocal part of the lens, which is for close-up sight. This may cause one to misjudge the height and trip. Since our ability to judge

depth (depth perception) decreases as we age, special attention should be applied under this circumstance. Walking can no longer be something we don't think about—it needs to be deliberate.

RECOMMENDATION: It is important to have your vision checked on a regular basis to make sure you are seeing the best that you can.

Inner Ear

Like vision, the inner ear's main job is to send information to the brain as to the whereabouts of your head relative to your body. The inner ear allows the brain to know the position of our head, whether upright, as in standing, rotated, tilted or horizontal, as in lying down. As we grow older, there is a greater risk for the inner ear to have problems. Many times, there is a mixed signal between one ear and the other. When this occurs, the brain becomes confused and unable to decipher which ear is telling it the truth. The resulting dizziness is what doctors call 'vertigo'.

Some other conditions that can cause vertigo include central nervous system disorders like Stroke, Parkinson's disease, and Otto toxicity (toxicity of the inner ear). There are also certain medications that can become toxic to the inner ear. As the toxicity in the inner ear builds, the inner ears ability to function correctly deteriorates. Thankfully, there are cures for many causes of vertigo. Any type of dizziness or vertigo requires the attention of a doctor that specializes in this area. This type of physician called as a **vestibular specialist** and the best way to locate one is to ask with your primary care physician.

RECOMMENDATION: It is important to have your ears checked on a regular basis to make sure that this part of your balance system is operating correctly. Be pro-active!

Sensory Component (Body Awareness)

The third component of your balance system is called "somatosensory". 'Somato' means body and 'sensory' means to send. These are nerve endings located in your joints and skin. For example, skin sensors in the soles of your feet allow you to feel the pressure of your body's weight. Joint receptors in ankles, knees and hips, let your brain know where your legs are relative to your body. In unison, these receptors play a powerful role in maintaining balance. Less pressure and changes in ankle position tell your brain your foot is no longer supporting your weight.

This valuable information then allows the brain to respond in order to keep you on your feet.

Often, police test this component of the balance system when putting someone through a sobriety test. Most of us have seen on television or on the street, a police officer asking an individual to close his or her eyes (taking the dominating visual component away), then telling them to bring their finger to their nose. The officer can tell, through this activity, if this sensory system is impaired.

To recap, as we grow older cellular function slows and therefore, one's ability to sense joint changes and skin pressure decreases. Likewise, as we age, certain diseases can compromise one's sensation or feeling. Diabetes, peripheral neuropathy, spinal stenosis, stroke, and arthritis are common culprits in this area. However, lack of proper nutrition and hydration, and vitamin deficiencies in individuals may also cause one to exhibit symptoms of peripheral neuropathy.

Probably the biggest culprit to a compromise in the somatosensory system is inactivity. By not getting up and walking regularly, the receptors become sluggish in their performance. The somatosensory component plays a big role in your brain's ability to process information before deciding what to do to maintain balance. Once it has made that decision, it will send orders to the muscles to turn on. This "motor planning" is better known as agility and coordination, and is the fourth component of one's balance system.

> **RECOMMENDATION:** For individuals with somatosensory loss through disease or inactivity, it is important to have your home inspected for safety hazards such as throw rugs on the floors and to be properly fitted with an appropriate walker or cane. Refer to the Home Safety Checklist in the Appendix.

Agility and Coordination

If you have had a stroke or know someone who has, you may know that one side of their body is affected. Depending on the severity of the stroke, the amount of time lapsed before medical attention, and the aggressiveness of their rehabilitation program, this paralysis can be temporary or permanent. This happens because a portion of the brain that controls the nerves to one side is damaged by the stroke. Other diseases that can affect nerves that go to our muscles are Parkinson's, Multiple Sclerosis, and other central nervous system disorders.

Simply stated, coordination is the ability of the brain to turn on and turn off muscles at the precise moment to create specific movements. Take for instance, walking. In order for one to walk, he has to be able to coordinate the muscles of the legs to fire and relax at precisely the right time, in order to mobilize his body forward. We have all seen a baby learning how to do this very task. It is amazing to see them develop coordination; it takes several months to perfect. As we perfect a movement, our brain stores the movement in what is known as motor memory. The more often we train at a certain task, the more engrained this motor pattern becomes.

> **RECOMMENDATION:** Agility and coordination can only improve with movement. By performing the dynamic balance program outlined in this book, you will be well on your way to engraining the movement programs necessary for safe balance. Remember to check with your healthcare provider before you begin this or any exercise program.

Strength

Your balance can only be as stable as the strength and stamina you have in your legs. We know that the only way we can make a muscle stronger is by using it, challenging it, having it contract against loads that are more than normal. Inactivity places a person at high risk for falling, the more sedentary a person is, the higher his risk for fall. However, there are also certain diseases that cause one to lose strength (muscle mass). Most of them fall under the category of neuromuscular disorders, like Parkinson's, stroke, Multiple Sclerosis, and Diabetes. These types of diseases cause your muscles to lose nerve signals resulting in weakness and loss of muscle function. Likewise, arthritis and related conditions are a precursor to one's lack of activity.

> **RECOMMENDATION:** Exercise, exercise, exercise (see the routines in this guide for exercise advice specific to developing good balance). Whether land based or in the water, a combination of, range of motion, stretching, strengthening and cardiovascular elements should be included in your exercise program. Exercising the brain is just as important—don't ever stop learning! There are a great number of community based exercise programs available for all ages and also for those with chronic disease. Seek them out and stick to them, you will be glad you did.

Posture

The final component in the balance system is posture, which is related to flexibility. I believe posture to be the biggest culprit of balance loss for those of advanced age. Soft tissue structures, like muscle, fascia and skin adjust to the position they are placed in all day.

For a large part of your day, you may be in a seated position. Many, who sit most of the day, find their legs become rigid and stiff, being unable to straighten their knees all the way upon rising. When they do stand, it looks as if they are in a sitting position standing up. Their muscles, tendons, ligaments, fascia, nerves, and skin all have assumed a certain length; length far less than what is functional.

Because of this state, they may walk with their head forward and forward rounded shoulders. This posture places most of the weight in front of their body, out side of their feet (their base of support). With one's body weight on the front of the foot, rather than centered and balanced properly over the foot, they become highly prone to falling forward. The average adult head weighs as much as a bowling ball. Imagine the effect of holding out a balling ball over your body all day—no wonder neck and back pain are so prevalent and balance is off.

Advancing age and chronic degenerative disease also play a role in one's posture. Probably the biggest culprit for poor posture in individuals of advancing age is lack of activity or exercise. When we are inactive, we allow muscles to weaken and atrophy, thereby causing a balance problem and increasing fall risk.

> **RECOMMENDATION:** Be as physically as active as possible. Incorporate the stretch program from this book into your daily exercise routine. In most cases, you can better your posture with exercise, and especially, awareness. Tai Chi and Yoga provide wonderful balance and stretching movements as well as bring awareness to your body. The saying is true. *"Use it or lose it"*. This is the case with your agility and your coordination as well as your overall strength and balance.
>
> **Precaution: In some instances, certain types of exercise movements may be contraindicative to your condition. If you have a chronic or degenerative condition or have had recent surgery, it is important to consult with your physician before beginning an exercise program.**

All six components of balance work closely with one another. We have broken them out in this book to show significance of each component and its special duty. In truth, they are intertwined into a single, working system. These components, when combined, make up the strength of your balance. For many, either one or two of these components begin to fail, as we grow older. Once we have become weak in one component, we find our balance becomes weak as well. The good news is that four of the six components involve your body and can usually be conditioned, regardless of the disease process being experienced. With a simple exercise program that takes just minutes a day, you can strengthen your balance system. Moreover, as you condition those components that are not affected by disease, you will notice improvement as the system as a whole adapts and conditions to use what is available.

Remember the study mentioned earlier of the young athletes who tasked with walking on a treadmill without the use of their vision? If you recall, not one of them was able to walk on the treadmill without their vision. Well the study did not end there. They took those same athletes and had them practice repeatedly walking on the treadmill without their vision. In just six weeks, all were able walk without falling. How did this happen? The body adapted to being able to balance without vision by conditioning the other components of the system to make up for the loss of vision.

The same could happen for you. If you have a disease or pathology that has taken one of your balance components away, there is hope. With the right kind of conditioning, you can condition the other components of the system to make up for what is not working. Exercises for increasing flexibility, strength and endurance are described later on in this text. Please know, that the more you do, the more you can do. Exercise and balance control is a big part of fall prevention.

The Golden Rule to Walking

After evaluating hundreds of patients gait patterns, I have come to realize the best thing we can do to prevent a fall when walking is to bring your heel down first when making that initial contact with the floor. In fact, this is the normal walking model and if you were to watch people walk you would find, that usually, the heel of their shoe hits the floor first. I have termed this the golden rule to walking because when you place your heel down first, you have more control over your forward momentum.

Think of it this way, walking is nothing more than a controlled fall that propels you forward. By stepping forward, you move your body's weight forward, outside of your base of support. If you did not put your heel down, you would keep falling forward until you landed flat on your face. In essence, that is what happens when we trip or catch a toe. We are unable to get our foot out in front of us in time to catch our body's forward momentum. When walking, you actually stop forward momentum before it is too late. In addition, in a normal walking pattern, when an individual takes a step, the heel is first part of their foot to make contact with the ground. The heel becomes a brake, and stops the fall.

When teaching this concept, many people walk away with a renewed sense of confidence in their walking ability because they now understand **how** to control their forward momentum. Simply put, the golden rule to walking is when you step out; make sure you come down on your heel first. Your heel is your natural brake; it allows you to stop your momentum from moving too far forward thereby creating a fall.

> **RECOMMENDATION:** Step out in front and come down on your heel first when walking. If you are unable to come down on your heel first, there is a good chance you may need daily exercise or a physical therapist to help condition your balance system.

Mobility

If you or a loved one utilizes a walker, cane, or wheelchair to be mobile, please note that most adaptive equipment adjusts to accommodate a variety of body types and physical conditions. I have personally witnessed some of my exercise students using canes that are adjusted far too short for their height, causing them to lean forward more than they would normally. They did not realize the cane was not adjusted properly for their height. Posturally speaking, if you don't adjust the cane or walker to fit your body height, you may be doing yourself more harm than good!

Visit a store that specializes in Medical Supplies or Durable Medical Equipment (DME), the staff should be able to help you adjust your mobility equipment to suit your body type and situation. They should also be able to teach you the correct use of the equipment. There is a 'right and wrong' way to use a cane, proper technique creates a much safer environment. There are now many different types and styles of canes and walkers. Canes come in single, triple or quad prong, each providing a different level of stability. Walkers now are as diverse as automobiles in model style and type. It is worth researching which one is right for your needs before investing.

If you need an adaptive or mobility device, get one! Having an assistive device doesn't mean you are weak—it means you are pro-active in helping yourself. Note, however, that the use of equipment, like walkers and canes may necessitate the changing of the configuration of some of your home surroundings for safety purposes.

If you have trouble getting out of bed, get a handrail for the bedside—they are inexpensive (about $100) and can stabilize you and help save you from falling out of bed when getting up in the middle of the night to use the restroom.

Grab bars in the bathroom are necessary, as getting into and out of the shower or tub requires you to be on one foot during entrance and exit. **Note that towel**

racks are not secured in the same way as grab bars and are not made to support the weight of a person! See the home safety checklist at the end of the book for room-by-room suggestions.

> **RECOMMENDATION:** Have friends and family help you with the cost and installation of home modifications. How about having a 'Home Safety' day where your family comes over to install small modifications that can dramatically reduce the fall risk in your home. You can also contact your local senior center or area 'Agency on Aging' and inquire about home modification programs they may sponsor.

Without a walker or cane, the average person needs about a 28" wide space to walk through a hall or doorway comfortably. With a walker or cane, that space increases to 36" to 42" in width. Accommodating this new need will keep the frustration and anxiety levels lower as you will not feel the need to 'navigate' through your own home. Additionally, fall risk will be lowered because you have been pro-active in creating a safer space in which to move.

Mobility issues do not negate the value of exercise. In fact, exercise can help in more ways than just physically. Studies show that people who exercise regularly have lower rates of depression, experience less chronic pain and have a generally more positive outlook on life. It's those endorphins! You don't need to be a marathon runner to experience feeling great after exercise. For many people the social interaction they get from participating in an exercise class is the most important and uplifting part of their day.

How does this relate to lowering your fall risk? Ask yourself, which person would be at less risk of falling—the depressed person, who is inactive, sedentary and has a negative outlook on life? On the other hand, would, the active, social person who has friends and experiences new situations on a regular basis be at more risk? My money is on the second person. How about yours? Odds are the first person may be taking more medication as well!

The Relationship of Medications and the Risk of Falls

Author: Patricia-Jo Dean, RN, C,
Contributions by: Joanne Price

BLOOD THINNER X 4!

It is vital that you are knowledgeable about the medications you take and the effects they have on your body and mind. Here is a story to demonstrate the importance of being aware of what you ingest.

After providing a Fall Prevention Seminar, one of the participants asked me about why he bruised so easily even though he had not fallen. I asked him if he was taking any blood thinning medications. He said, "Yes he was taking Coumadin." *(blood thinner #1).*

I then asked if he was taking any over the counter medications, he said he had been taking a baby aspirin every day because he had read it was good for his heart *(blood thinner #2).* I then asked if he was taking any herbal supplements or vitamins. He said yes, a multi-vitamin and a specially concentrated garlic tablet that was "good for his blood" *(blood thinner #3).*

I asked if he drank alcohol. He said he had a glass of wine with dinner in the evening *(blood thinner #4).* This man, thinking he was doing all good things for his body was actually taking **FOUR** blood thinners each day! It is no wonder that he bruised so easily. He did not realize the combined effects of the medication, the over the counter aspirin, supplement and alcohol were creating a very dangerous situation. My recommendation was that he should call his doctor to discuss the situation—immediately!

Nobody can know everything, but I encourage you to become as knowledgeable as possible regarding the subject matter presented in this book—for your own well-being and for the well-being of people you care for.

THE MEDICATION CONNECTION

Do medications contribute to fall risk? This is a complex question without a blanket answer. Instead, one might ask, "Do my medications contribute to my risk of falling?" Before you can answer that question, you should first review the medications (prescription and over the counter) and supplements you consume. Fall risk can be affected by the use of prescription medications and by the use of, and interaction between, prescription medications, over the counter (OTC) medications and supplements.

Approximately one out of three adults over the age of 65 experience a fall annually. Falls and the resulting injuries can be serious and sometimes life threatening. Sadly, several thousand seniors lose their lives each year because of a fall or complications resulting from their injuries.

Over the past several years, the number of newly available medications for chronic conditions has increased significantly. The availability of these new treatments has contributed to the use of multiple medications, especially in the senior population. The average older adult is taking at least four different medications. The more medications one uses, the greater the risk of an adverse (unwanted) effect, such as a loss of balance or a fall.

Some studies show that the **potential** for an adverse side effect is about 6% when an individual takes two drugs. When five drugs are used, that **potential** increases at 50% and if eight or more medications are being taken, the **potential** for an adverse side effect is 100%.

The example, is from a recent article by Gregory Gahm, MD, in *Advance* magazine it describes how a previously healthy adult can quickly become someone taking multiple medications and be at 100% risk of an adverse effects of the medications (refer to the study findings above).

> *"An individual has mild arthritis and starts taking an NSAID (anti-inflammatory) medication. This type of medication can cause fluid retention, resulting*

in edema (swelling of the legs). *The individual is now prescribed a diuretic (water pill) and potassium. The medications became irritating to the patient's stomach and the doctor prescribes medicine to reduce the gastric acid, but not before some bleeding of the stomach lining occurs because of the irritation.*

The bleeding causes the doctor to order Iron supplements and due to the constipation caused by the Iron, the person now needs a stool softener and laxative. The individual is understandably depressed over the situation and is prescribed an antidepressant. **This previously healthy senior is now taking 12 pills a day."**

Does this story sound familiar? This situation takes place more than you might think. When any new medication, including over the counter medications are added to your medication regimen, careful monitoring should be done to ensure the medications are used according to the doctor's recommendations. We will talk next about some of the ways you can reduce your risk of falls by becoming educated on the medications you take and the side effects that could be experienced while taking specific types of medication. Through knowing what side effects can be, it may be more likely that you will adapt your surroundings to provide you additional safety in case of a fall due to a side effect. Knowledge is power only if you take action!

WHAT'S IN A NAME?

One of the most important factors in the safe use of medications is to know the names and dosages of each medication you take. Also important are the reason(s) the medication is used and any potential side effects. The best way to keep track of your medication is to have a list for reference at home and in your purse or wallet to show when you visit a doctor.

Many older adults have more than one doctor, each of whom may prescribe medications. Whenever you visit a doctor make sure he or she reviews your medication list and updates your medical record. This a simple way to ensure that the doctor is aware of all current medications and, orders medications (when necessary) that are safely taken together with the others you are currently receiving.

Another resource that is readily available to assist you in monitoring medications is your pharmacist. If it is possible to fill your prescriptions at the same pharmacy, may be beneficial as well. Most pharmacy computers have a list of all the medications that have been filled for each customer at their store and may have a list of allergies (if previously provided). If all of your prescriptions are filled at the same drug store, the pharmacist is usually alerted when medications are ordered that may cause unwanted side effects when taken together with the others currently prescribed. Usually, the pharmacist will assist you by calling your doctor to discuss the problem. The doctor may decide to change the medication or if she determines that the unwanted effects are mild and you are aware to report any problems, she may tell the pharmacist to fill the prescription.

> **RECOMMENDATION:** Bring an up to date list of prescription medications, OTC medications and supplements you take to your doctor and pharmacist when you visit. Request a 'medication review'. This review will not only remind the doctor of what you are taking but will also help you to learn more about the side effects of your medication regimen.

When you use the above recommendation, at least three individuals will be aware and can help you to monitor your medications (you, the doctor and the pharmacist). For many older adults there is also a trusted family member or friend who may help to organize your medications. If needed, enlist their help in learning more about the effects and possible side effects of your medications as well. If you don't have someone to help you, hiring a care manager or home care agency could be of benefit. If you are alone, be as knowledgeable as possible about your medications.

> **RECOMMENDATION:** Take a friend or caregiver with you to the doctor and to the pharmacy next time you go. This way you have two sets of ears hearing about your medication changes and any potential side effects.

It is worth noting, that sometimes medication is not needed to treat certain conditions. Diet and lifestyle adjustments such as reducing sodium intake, joining a senior wellness group for exercise and social interaction, or a "clean sweep" of clutter from the home can improve general well being and decrease the risk of falls. When you visit the doctor, ask if there are other approaches, aside from the use of long-term medications, that you can incorporate into your daily activities, which may enable the doctor to order a lower dosage or eliminate the need for the medication.

EFFECT OR SIDE EFFECT?

The *effect* of medication is the desired change caused by the medication, for instance, a lowering of the blood pressure to a 'normal' level or relief of arthritic pain. A *side effect* is an effect that may occur as a result of the medication but is not the intended effect. A side effect may be minor, although perhaps uncomfortable, such as nausea for a day or two while your system adjusts to the medication. A side effect also can be of major concern, such as confusion, dizziness or excessive drowsiness.

Your doctor, their nurse or physician's assistant should inform you of any side effects of concern. Any problem is important to report to the doctor so that she can determine if the side effect is serious and requires intervention. The result may be as simple as the doctor recommending that you take the medication at a different time.

Another type of effect of medications is called an *adverse effect*, such as an allergic reaction. These effects are not usually common and any concerns should be reported immediately to a doctor. The more you educate yourself on the *effects, side effects and possible adverse effects* of your medications, the more in control you will feel.

MEDICATION COMPLIANCE

Let's say, your medications are ordered and you are educated as to their names, function and dosages. Now, following the schedule ordered by the doctor (for example; once a day, before meals, or bedtime) is the next important factor to review. Research has shown that seventy-five percent of seniors do not follow the recommended medication regimen. Some of the reasons reported are:

- Uncomfortable side effects;
- Feelings that the medication is not working or not needed any longer and;
- The high cost of medications;
- Taking medications until they feel a little better, then stopping.

- Becoming forgetful or confused as to when the last dosage was taken, thereby omitting a dose or doubling up.

RECOMMENDATIONS:

- Contact your healthcare provider; they may be able to suggest an alternative schedule or dosage.

- Create a written schedule and check off when taken.

- Organize medications in reminder containers—inexpensive and easy to do. If you are having difficulty organizing medications, request the help of a family member, trusted friend or caregiver.

- Ask your pharmacist about less expensive alternatives.

- Ask your Area Agency on Aging for alternative medication programs.

- Keep medications in the same place all the time.

- Ask the Pharmacy staff to print your instructions and side effects in large size print for you.

As in all things, your knowledge is power if you are proactive with your knowledge, including lowering fall risk.

REVIEW OF SOME COMMON TYPES OF MEDICATIONS

IMPORTANT: This section is not meant to be all-inclusive. We intend to motivate you to be pro-active in learning about your medications and to urge you to consult your healthcare provider about how you can minimize negative side effects and lower your risk of falls.

High blood pressure medication (anti-hypertensive)

The **desired effect** of medication used for high blood pressure is to lower the blood pressure (BP) to a safe level, reduce the work of the heart and to prevent other damaging effects of persistent high blood pressure.

Medications used to treat high blood pressure are known as anti-hypertensive's. The way they control BP can be different for each type of anti-hypertensive.

Some work to reduce the resistance of the blood vessels and relax arterial muscles while others decrease the amount of blood the heart pumps each time (reducing amount of work the heart needs to do to pump blood). Others affect the adrenal glands by blocking agents that send the body signals to increase the blood pressure.

In addition to the medication, lifestyle changes may help to manage high blood pressure. Stop smoking, avoid alcohol and limiting salt intake have been shown to be quite helpful. Excess body weight is also a factor in high BP. Increasing physical activity with a doctor-approved program will help reduce body fat and work to reduce stress as well.

The following list, although not all-inclusive, details some of the side effects of anti-hypertensive medications that can contribute to fall risk:

- Low blood pressure, which may worsen when rising from a lying or seated position (Orthostatic hypotension).

RECOMMENDATION: Rise slowly from lying and sit on the side of bed or sofa for a few minutes before standing. Risk of falling increases if you stand too quickly.

- Dizziness or becoming light headed may also be connected to rising too quickly, or heat.

- Dehydration (some blood pressure medications are combined with diuretics also known as water pills), dehydration can also cause dizziness, confusion and further lowering of blood pressure which increases the risk of falls.

RECOMMENDATION: Have water handy at all times. Rest when needed, do not over-exert. Seek out 'safe zones' in your community that have air-conditioning when the weather really heats up.

- Fainting (syncope) can occur as a result of any of the side effects listed above and is an obvious cause of falls. Since, with loss of consciousness, the senior cannot break the fall and possibly avoid serious injury.

RECOMMENDATION: Avoid prolonged standing, especially in very warm environments. Sit or lie down if you feel faint. Alert bystanders so they can assist you. Report fainting or dizziness to your doctor as soon as possible.

Rise slowly from lying. Sit on the side of the bed for a few minutes before standing. This may reduce the risk of falling from plummeting blood pressure caused by rising too quickly.

'Water Pills' or 'Fluid Pills' (diuretics)

The desired effect of a diuretic is to prevent or reduce excess build up of fluid in the body, which causes, for instance, swelling in the legs. There are several causes of excess fluid retention that your doctor should explain to you. Some of the side effects of diuretic medications may include:

- Urinary urgency, the need to go to the bathroom immediately or else become incontinent. Rising quickly to hurry to the bathroom-a sure increase of the risk of tripping and falling.

RECOMMENDATIONS:

- Try to use the bathroom on a more frequent basis, rather than wait for the urge to overwhelm you and cause you to hurry. Learn and practice 'Kegal' Exercises (see the 'Progression and More' section of this book.)

- Remove clutter and anything that blocks a clear path to the bathroom.

- Avoid wearing very long or loose bed clothing that might become tangled in bedding.

- Have a lit path to the bathroom.

- Electrolyte imbalance, a change in the mineral elements that keep your heart and other organs healthy and functioning can be lost in the urine when taking certain diuretics. Electrolyte imbalance can cause muscle weakness and confusion (in addition to other problems). Again, adding to ones risk for falls.

RECOMMENDATION: Discuss taking a potassium supplement, orange juice or banana with your doctor to replace the potassium lost with frequent urination. This may help electrolyte imbalance.

RECOMMENDATION: Be sure to use your eyeglasses as prescribed. When walking or driving in sunny areas or areas with snow, use prescription sunglasses. Report eyesight changes to your doctor. They may interfere with your performance of normal daily activities. Take time when you move from a darkened area to a light room or vice versa. This will allow your eyes to get used to the change in lighting, helping you see more clearly. As we age, it takes our eyes longer to focus, know this and take the few extra moments to focus; it may save your life. Ensure adequate lighting all around your home (another way to help prevent falls).

Heart (cardiovascular) medications

- Low blood pressure (once again a recurring theme)

RECOMMENDATION: Nitroglycerin can cause this quickly, if you have angina and need to take a "Nitro", be seated first, so if your blood pressure decreases quickly you will be safer than if you are standing.

- Elevated levels in the blood (such as with Digoxin) can cause visual disturbances and changes in mental status, putting an individual at risk for falls. The doctor may order blood testing to be done.

Anti-depressant medications and other types of psychotropic medications

These medications are used to treat mood or cognitive problems caused by medical conditions including stroke, Parkinson's disease and dementia, as well as others.

- Low blood pressure

- Dizziness

- Blurred vision

- Sedation, mild sedation may occur at the start of antidepressant therapy and will usually resolve after a few days.

RECOMMENDATIONS:

- Ask the doctor if the medication can be taken at night, which may decrease sedation during the day.

- If the sedation is more than mild, notify the doctor immediately.

- Initial monitoring of the patient by a friend, family member or caregiver is recommended as they are at higher risk of falls during this time.

• Driving is inadvisable.

Anti-Parkinson medications

• Low blood pressure

• Syncope

• Increased tremors can occur after a length of treatment time, which increases the already unsteady gait of an individual with Parkinson's disease and increasing the fall risk.

Pain (analgesic) medications (other than anti-inflammatory medications)

• Drowsiness, usually temporary, but may decrease attention to tasks and decrease in safety awareness putting you at risk for falls.

• Sedation

• Change in mental status, confusion

Laughter

Happily, there are absolutely no side effects from laughter except maybe an occasional 'stitch' in your side. Laughter is also good for your internal organs and abdominal muscles. Remember the saying 'Laughter is the best medicine' and try a dose each day!

As you have now learned, many of the most commonly used types of medications can cause an increased risk of falls. The risk of adverse effects, including falls, increases dramatically with the use of multiple medications. By increasing your awareness of the medications prescribed, the effects desired and the side effects to watch for, you can reduce your risk (or that of someone you care about) and minimize of the possible devastating life changing effects of falls.

Not every medication has the desired effect on every person. There are times, especially with high blood pressure and pain medications, where the doctor may need to try more than one medication to treat the problem. She will order one at a time and monitor you for the desired effect. If the medication is not working for you, she may discontinue it and try another. This process is not unusual when a patient is initially diagnosed with a problem, such as high blood pressure.

If a medication is not effective or you feel that you no longer need it, discuss it with the doctor rather than abruptly stopping. In some cases, abruptly stopping a medication can cause other unwanted side effects. Of course, any signs of allergy or other symptoms that concern you should be immediately reported to the doctor.

> **RECOMMENDATION:** Do an occasional "spring cleaning" of your medicine chest to remove medication that you are no longer prescribed or has expired. If you are inadvertently using some of these expired medications, they may be too old to be effective and, possibly, unsafe to consume. Crushing or chewing some medications can reduce or eliminate the effectiveness of the drug. Always follow the instructions provided with the medication and those written on the container. Be sure to ask your pharmacist if you have any concerns. **Instructions and side effect information can be printed in a large size font for you, but you need to make that request.**

Some medications can affect your balance, bone density, your appetite, thirst response, blood pressure, and digestive or elimination process. Your power lies in the knowledge you possess and the control you implement regarding your medications and the effects they have on your body.

RECOMMENDATION REVIEW

- Stay organized, in home and in health.
- Exercise (if organized exercise classes are not your style, exercise tapes are easy and inexpensive and you can start and stop them at your convenience. You can even 'mute' the sound! Go to your local library and check one out for a minimal cost. Our local library charges only $1.00 per week to check out exercise videos.
- Learn and practice 'Kegal' Exercises (very important and useful for urinary issues, see exercise section of this book).
- Eat healthy—even if you don't feel like it.
- Drink enough water to appropriately metabolize your medications and keep your body functioning properly. Read specific recommen-

dations in the chapter on Nutrition and Hydration found in this book.

- Drink majority of water before 5-6 pm if experiencing frequent nighttime bathroom needs.

- Bring a friend to doctor visits, ask questions about side effects of medications.

- Have your medications reviewed periodically. See medication review form included in this guide for a template.

- Write down problems when they occur so that they can be addressed at your next office visit (or sooner if needed).

- Keep a list of current medications and health conditions on your refrigerator and have a copy on your person when out.

Lastly, remember that doctors and other healthcare providers are people too, they are not perfect and they always appreciate a proactive patient. Be involved in your own care and learn as much as possible about your condition(s) and the medications that you have been prescribed. You have the power to help heal your body through proactive behaviors and treating yourself well physically, nutritionally, mentally and spiritually.

Dietary Habits and Risk of Falls

Author: Joanne Price
Contributions and Review: Amy McAllister, Registered Dietitian

THE IMPORTANCE OF HYDRATION

Many older adults over 65 are dehydrated and malnourished. Unfortunately, as we age we may experience a decreased sense of thirst. Lack of hydration can display itself in a number of ways, including a slower metabolism, decreased clarity of thought, decreased hunger and constipation. Constipation can increase toxicity in our bodies, and have devastating effects including causing memory impairment! Our bodies need water to survive. We can see a correlation between nutrition, hydration and fall risk directly by looking at the effect that dehydration and lack of good nutrition have on our bodies.

REASONS FOR DECREASED FLUID INTAKE:

- Decreased thirst sensation
- Difficulty swallowing
- Decreased bladder control
- Forgetting to drink

Due to the decrease in 'thirst' response, it is important to remind yourself and those you care about to drink water and track hydration as you do your medications. Medications cannot do their job if the body does not process them. Hydration is the key to proper assimilation of nutrients and medications and to the removal of toxins and waste from your system.

RECOMMENDATIONS:

- Log your water intake, if you find yourself getting up too many times in the night to use the bathroom, consume the majority of your liquids prior to 5pm.

- Try flavored waters or tea (non-caffeinated); add a squeeze of lemon or orange.

- Dilute juices with water or seltzer, to decrease sugar and calories and make your juices last longer. This will hydrate you more than a full strength juice.

- Limit your intake of caffeinated beverages.

- Check with your doctor, dietitian or pharmacist on types of juice you should or should not have—some medications react adversely with certain fruit (i.e. grapefruit and grapefruit juice should not be consumed when prescribed certain medications).

- Drink 6-8 oz. of water or water-juice with each medication dosage (this will not only help with metabolizing the medication but with your hydration quota as well).

- Drink the majority of water prior to 5pm.

Water helps clean out the system, removing toxins, promoting good digestion and stimulating appetite. Lack of water can cause one to become disoriented, contributing to an increase in fall risk. Dehydration and malnutrition can cause dizziness, loss of balance and general weakness.

At a recent meeting of health care administrators, a physician who was discussing the problem of urinary infections in older adults living in assisted living and skilled nursing facilities. He pointed out that some residents who were exhibiting signs of dementia, had reversed the symptoms when treated for dehydration and an underlying urinary tract infection. Hydration is serious business and is easily dealt with—all you need to do is drink water!

THE ROLE OF NUTRITION

As we age, eating a nutritious diet is extremely important. Although caloric needs may decrease as we age, nutritional requirements may increase. There have been recent studies correlating increased Vitamin D consumption with a decreased risk of falls. Nutritional decline and dehydration both cause an increase in potential risk for falls in the older adult population. Malnutrition can cause vitamin, electrolyte, protein, and other deficiencies. Many older adults do not receive adequate nutrition, now that microwaves rule the kitchen; we don't even smell the food cooking. Smelling food being prepared also stimulates appetite. Think about the smell of a great meal and dessert being prepared in your kitchen, it will make your mouth water. Saliva aids in good digestion. Some causes of poor nutrition for senior citizens include:

- Loss of taste and smell due to illness or medications
- Poor dental health, loss of teeth, and ill fitting dentures cause difficulty chewing
- Swallowing difficulties
- Arthritis or other physical conditions which make grocery shopping and meal preparation more difficult
- Loneliness and depression
- Inactivity
- Financial considerations
- Not physically able to 'cook'
- Unappetizing or unclean environment or food presentation

Let's face it, if you're not hungry, it may be difficult to coax yourself into cooking, eating, and cleaning up after a meal. In addition, the actual act of eating day-after-day does not hold much interest for many people living alone. The process of meal preparation holds a social connotation for most of us and 'breaking bread' alone is just not motivating.

RECOMMENDATIONS:

- Many senior centers and churches serve senior lunches for a nominal charge; many even provide transportation and enjoyable educational programming before or after the meal.
- Invite a neighbor—share the preparation. You will find yourself looking forward to your day to prepare and share. Make plans to not eat alone when possible. Just the socialization alone is worth the effort and is good for your overall health.
- Cook real food. Many prepared frozen dishes are high in salt, fresh is best.

- If you have trouble chewing, steam veggies until soft or create a fresh puree that goes great over pasta or as a soup.

- Get a juicer! Fresh fruit/veggie juice is one of the best and most nutritious drinks you could consume.

- 'Meals on Wheels' is available in most areas. Call for your area information. The folks that deliver the meals are very nice and you will find yourself looking forward to that friendly 'knock on the door'.

- Share grocery trips to the store. Both physically and monetarily. If you think getting a whole head of lettuce is too much, split it with a neighbor. Buy in larger quantities to save money and divide the groceries.

Use the following guidelines to develop a good nutritional program for yourself or someone you care for:

NUTRITION & HYDRATION REQUIREMENTS

Protein: 1.0 to 1.2 g Pro/kg body weight for healthy individuals
15-20% of total caloric intake should come from protein.

Fat: 30% of total caloric intake should come from fat
No more than 10% of fat intake should be saturated or hydrogenated.

Carbohydrates: 45-50% of total caloric intake needs to come from carbohydrates, and half of carbohydrate intake should be from whole grains. Remember, fruits and vegetables are a source of carbohydrate.

Calories: Individual calorie needs are based on basal metabolic rate (BMR is the amount of energy expended while at rest), and individual activity level. There is a 10% reduction of caloric needs between ages 51-75, with an additional 10-15% reduction after the age of 75 depending on activity level.

Fiber: Fiber intake should be 20-35 grams per day. Fiber should be increased gradually, with adequate fluid intake to decrease gastric discomfort.

Vitamin A: Need decreases; avoid supplements containing vitamin A.

Vitamin D: Need increases; get some exposure to sunlight when possible (unless recommended otherwise by a physician) and include vitamin D-rich foods, such as fish and vitamin D fortified skim milk, in the diet. Discuss Vitamin D supplements with physician

Vitamin B12: Needs increase; eat vitamin B12-rich foods, such as lean red meat, chicken, and skim milk

Chromium: Needs increase; increase intake of foods high in chromium, such as brewer's yeast and whole grain

Zinc: Need increases; eat foods rich in zinc, such as lean red meat, oysters, wheat germ and whole grains

Water: 6.5 to 8 cups daily fluid, or approximately 30 cc/kg weight, more if you are very active.

GUIDELINES FOR A HEALTHY DIET

Mix up your choices within each food group.

- **Focus on fruits.** Eat a variety of fruits—whether fresh, frozen, canned, or dried—rather than fruit juice for most of your fruit choices. For a 2,000-calorie diet, you will need 2 cups of fruit each day (for example, one small banana, 1 large orange, and 1/4 cup of dried apricots or peaches). Please note that dried fruits contain a much higher concentration of sugar.

- **Vary your veggies.** Eat more dark green veggies, such as broccoli, kale, and other dark leafy greens; orange veggies, such as carrots, sweet potatoes, pumpkin, and winter squash.

- **Get your calcium-rich foods.** Get 3 cups of low fat or fat-free milk—or an equivalent amount of low-fat yogurt and/or low-fat cheese (1½ ounces of cheese equals 1 cup of milk)—every day. If you do not or cannot consume milk, choose lactose-free milk products and/or calcium-fortified foods and beverages.

- **Make at least half your grains whole.** Eat at least 3 ounces of whole-grain cereals, breads, crackers, rice, or pasta every day. One ounce is about one slice of bread, 1 cup of breakfast cereal, or ½ cup of cooked rice or pasta. Look to see that grains such as wheat, rice, oats, or corn are referred to as "whole" in the list of ingredients.

- **Go lean with protein.** Choose lean meats and poultry. Bake it, broil it, or grill it. Try to vary your protein choices—with more fish, beans, peas, nuts, and seeds.

Know the limits on fats, salt, and sugars. Read the 'Nutrition Facts' label on foods. Look for foods low in saturated fats and trans fats. Choose and prepare foods and beverages with little salt (sodium) and/or added sugars (caloric sweeteners).

Meal Pattern: Make sure to eat three meals daily with healthy between meal snacks. Small frequent meals will help to provide adequate calories, nutrients and fluids.

RECOMMENDATION: It is important to note that certain diseases and medications may warrant changes in dietary habits. Discuss the best approach for your particular situation with your healthcare provider who is aware of your individual requirements.

Home Safety

Author: Joanne Price, Fall Prevention Educator
CEO, Integricare Corporation

Is your home working for you or against you? The average home is built for a 'thirty something' couple with no children and no older adults. Our abode needs to be modified to accompany us safely through the different stages of our lives, including our golden years. Homes are not 'baby proof' when they are built, we adapt them to be safer for our children. We all know couples that have gone through the stage of placing covers on outlets and safety latches on cabinets for safety.

We view this as process as prudent and necessary to protect the well-being of the young members of our family. As we age, we need to look at the golden stage as one that also deserves attention in the home modification area to protect our safety, independence and wellbeing. Your home environment is stagnant. We need to change (adapt) the environment to create a safe home whether for children, grandchildren, friends or ourselves.

In this section, we address what you can do to lower fall risk and increase safety in each room of your home. As with this entire book, take what you need and leave the rest. Keep the book for future reference or give it to someone else who can benefit from the advice and information. Each person has a different set of circumstances and lifestyle. Adjust what you can, and don't get overwhelmed by attempting to do everything at once. Maybe this month you clear some clutter and next month have a grab bar or two installed. I learned a long time ago, that no job is too big, when broken down into small enough increments.

STARTING POINT

According to a recent study, when patients with recent fall history were provided a home visit with fall assessment, there was a 37% reduction in falls. Home assessments and home safety equipment are usually inexpensive and include easy-to-install items such as grab bars, raised toilet seats, shower seats and non-slip treads on steps. Some home modifications can be quite costly, as in remodeling a bathroom. For a complete list of recommended home modifications, see the Home Safety Checklist in the Appendix.

A simplified floor plan is recommended as well as pathway width increasing to 36" to 42" or more where needed. See the home safety checklist at the end of this book for suggestions. Items to look for when performing a home assessment include electrical cords (too many or frayed or crossing pathways), piles of books or newspapers on floor, cluttered counter space in any room, uneven or difficult stair steps, loose handrails and uneven flooring to name a few. Beloved pets pose a risk as well as they tend to be by the owner's feet. For someone already at risk, a loving cat could be the reason for a serious fall.

HOME MODIFICATION COSTS

The majority of falls occur at home. I firmly believe that if home safety were at the top of every family's list for aging parents and their community's older adult population, it would be possible to reduce falls significantly. Modifications include installing or verifying the integrity of stair railings and ramps, installation of grab bars inside and outside the shower for safe entry and exit. A bath seat and shower stall foot grips are very inexpensive and easy ways to help improve the safety factor for an older adult or someone with a chronic condition that affects their balance.

Home safety modifications can be of little or no cost to the resident. For example, with changes in furniture patterns (not always recommended, as pattern changes can create anxiety and fear in some older folks), elimination of floor hazards, increasing light bulb wattage, getting rid of clutter and ensuring safe electrical cord patterns can decrease in fall risk in a few hours of spring-cleaning!

Home modifications can also be quite costly as in the case of ramp installation or a bathroom remodel. County aging departments and community-based organizations often have handyman programs wherein the client pays only for materials. The labor is performed at no charge, thereby making ramps and grab bar installation possible for all who need them, no matter their financial situation.

RECOMMENDATION: Call your local senior center or area Agency on Aging to inquire about Home Modification programs available in your area. Some senior centers are located inside community centers. Don't give up—resources are available. Start by calling your local 'City Hall' and asking for a Senior Citizen Services representative.

Complete elimination of fall risk is probably not possible. No home and safety modifications in the world will eliminate fall risk in and of themselves. The other type of modification that is essential in order to lower risk of falls is **behavior modification**.

High fall risk behaviors include walking while performing any other type of activity like talking on the telephone, reading or watching TV. Not holding grab bars when entering or exiting the shower or climbing ladders, not paying attention to stairs and curbs and generally not being mindful create a high fall risk situation.

One particular risk, both inside and outside the home, is inappropriate footwear. Although it seems more prevalent inside the home when the individual takes off their supportive shoes worn when outside the home and replaces them with slippers or 'scuffies'. Improper footwear can be a problem both inside and outside the home. Non-supportive and loose slip-ons offer little or no support for the foot and often have no grip on the bottom, thus, increasing fall risk. Proper fitting moccasin style slippers with a good sole are more appropriate than oversized slippers and offer some support for the foot as well.

RECOMMENDATION: Become aware of your individual risky behaviors and use them to guide you as to what 'behavior modifications' will help to lower your risk of fall related injuries.

What If I Do Fall!

What if you do fall—then what? Getting help as quickly as possible is the priority. Using a medical alarm (press a necklace or wrist-based button, which calls for help) is of great benefit to get help quickly if you fall or experience any type of emergency where you are unable or afraid to get to a telephone. You should also have a telephone that is reachable from the floor on each level of your home, so if you do not have a medical alert button or are not wearing it at the time of the emergency you can possibly crawl to the phone and call for help.

ADDRESSING FEAR

The older we get, the more people we know who have fallen with serious consequences. Since it takes longer for wounds, bruises and broken bones to heal as we age, preventing falls should be an important goal in maintaining our health and independence. Unfortunately, the more stories we hear about our friends, neighbors and family falling, the more fearful we can become. With falls, it is important not to panic as this can actually make matters worse.

Although we do **NOT** recommend practice falling to rid ourselves of fear and 'get it right', visualizing surviving and successfully rising from a fall may be helpful in case it happens. As previously stated, by the age of 80, the likelihood of falling rises to almost 100%. This statistic alone should be enough to motivate all of us to be pro-active in our quest to decrease fall risk.

Surviving a fall accident not only depends on your action during the fall but your reaction after the event. For example, you may be familiar with this anecdote.

A drunk driver and a sober driver are in an auto accident, who gets hurt the worse? It seems the sober drivers sustain more significant injuries, doesn't it? One reason may be that the response time of the drunk driver is slow; therefore, they do not have time to panic. The sober driver, aware of what is happening, responds by stiffening all their muscles in panic.

Unfortunately, this act of stiffening the body will create a formula for sustaining more injuries. Trying to relax into the fall may very well protect you from serious injury. This is why visualization and review are important. In other words, go with the flow!

How you respond after you fall is just as important. You should have a 'plan of action' for yourself in case of an emergency. This is where our recommendation of a medical alert 'button' becomes important.

PERSONAL EMERGENCY RESPONSE SYSTEMS

Known as personal emergency response systems or PERS, 'medical alert buttons' or 'medical alarms', these devices are the most affordable and reliable 'plan of action' available for people who live alone or with someone who would be unable to get help if needed. For instance, a person living with someone with dementia who would be unable to call for help if his or her spouse or caregiver were to experience an emergency and be unable to call or assistance. Medical alarms are recommended by physicians, physical therapists, nurses, social workers, case managers and home care providers for safety and peace of mind.

With new technology, advancements incorporated into some brands of these units include unmonitored medication reminders, monitored medication compliance, fall detection (so you don't even have to press a button), daily wellness checks, contact of assistance in non-emergency situations, motion sensors and two-way voice communication with call center operators.

Usually waterproof, these pendant-based devices come with the pendant and a base unit. They provide peace of mind to the wearer, knowing they will receive help quickly in the event of an emergency by activating they system. However, these units are not fail-proof and have specific amount of area coverage of which the individual must be aware. Coverage area is determined by household layout and building materials. For example, the pendant signal cannot go through metal doors or foil wallpaper.

PERS systems range in price and features vary. The use of one of a PERS is encouraged for those with balance issues who are at risk for falls, those with chronic medical conditions, those living alone or those at risk of medical emergency (i.e., Diabetes, history of TIA's, Parkinson's). If you live alone, one of these pendant based buttons can provide peace of mind to you and your loved ones.

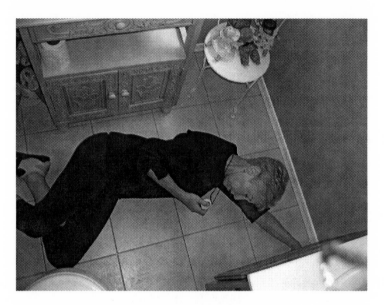

Luckily she has a medical alert button!

The waterproof button can be pressed to summon help for any type of emergency. Some people have pressed the button because of attempted robberies in progress or have smelled smoke. Whatever the reason, the call center operators will summon the appropriate help for you and stay on the line until help arrives.

There is usually an enrollment and installation fee (the total should not exceed $75) and a monthly monitoring fee (should not exceed $40/month). Find a local provider, who installs and tests the equipment for you, and can provide prompt and ongoing customer service. It is important to check the company out with the Better Business Bureau before moving forward with order placement. Avoid medical alert companies that require long-term contracts or significant up front fees. You will receive better customer service and faster results from service inquiries like replacement of lost pendants or batteries through using a local representative as opposed to a mail order.

PERS costs vary, averaging an installation fee of less than $75 and a monthly monitoring fee of less than $40 per month. Currently, Medicare does not cover medical alert systems, as they have been deemed 'non-therapeutic'. I hope that this will change in the future. Some long-term care policies do cover unit costs. Check with your insurance agent to see if your policy covers PERS. Ask about installation of a lockbox as well. Lockboxes assure that emergency personnel can enter a residence to render assistance quickly. Most companies offer options for wearing the pendant on the wrist or as a necklace.

> **RECOMMENDATION:** Have a medical alert system installed for your safety and peace of mind. For information on a PERS and to obtain additional fall prevention resources, contact Joanne Price (contact information found in the back of the book).

HIP PROTECTORS

Hip protectors are a great option for many people at risk for falls, especially those that are frail, have osteoporosis or have a history of falling. The undergarment is designed to be worn on the hips (pads slip into side pockets, looks like a girdle) to absorb and move energy away from the point of impact. Many DME's (durable medical equipment or medical supply) and pharmacy stores now carry hip protectors. They are utilized with great success in many assisted living communities. Hip protectors can be purchased at your local medical supply store.

> **RECOMMENDATION:** Search for 'hip protectors, elderly falls' online and results appear showing several mail order options as well. Some are disposable, many are washable and most are easy to wear and very comfortable. They can also be found at many Pharmacies and DME stores.

COMMUNITY BASED PROGRAMS

Many area Agencies on Aging (local and state departments on aging may have a different name in your area) have programs that provide an automated 'check up' on seniors on a daily basis. Some are known as 'We Are Not Alone' programs. This is one way to have an individual know that he would be found if he is unable to call for help. 'We Are Not Alone' are free programs and are often sponsored by volunteer police. Participation in a program is particularly valuable if an older adult does not have a large social circle, or lives in a rural area.

Exercises to Increase Balance

By: Brett Longo, PT
Contributions by: Joanne Price
Fitness Model: Linda Balducci

Let's use an example the individual who has poor flexibility in their hips, low back and knees, and postures with a rounded back and shoulders and a forward head. If they have been sitting for long periods of time, they probably are unable to fully straighten their knees because the hamstring muscles, found in back of the knee, become adjusted to the bent knee position of sitting, and they are unable to fully extend at the hip because their hip flexor muscles, found in front of the hip, have adjusted to the position their hips are in when sitting. When asked to stand, this individual is unable to fully stand erect and usually ends up in a stooped position. Moreover, when asked to walk, they end up walking flat footed or worse shuffling flat footed.

If you or someone you care about has this type of a posture and is unable to straighten their knees and/or hips with standing, then I have great news, you are likely only four stretches away from having your posture corrected. Correcting posture will decrease your risk for a fall. These stretches are easy to do and should be performed several times a week for best results.

GENERAL STRETCH PRINCIPLES TO FOLLOW

It is important to outline some general principles to follow to perform stretches correctly. First, you never want to stretch in a painful position. Often times we think that we really have to bear down and push on the muscle in order to get muscles and soft tissue to lengthen, but this type of a stretch actually can be hurtful to our muscles in that it can cause the muscle to tear.

Second, when you stretch, you want to come to a point of tension and hold. You do not want to bounce. Bouncing was popular many years ago but research shows that bouncing actually causes muscles to shorten instead of lengthen. So please do not bounce, come to a point of tension and hold.

Third, the length of time one holds a stretch is related to how flexible one can become. Although there is a genetic component to flexibility, most of us are more flexible than we realize, we just have not reached our full potential in this area.

The more often and the longer you hold a stretch position, the greater the benefit. Someone who can hold a stretched position for two to three minutes will benefit more so than someone who can hold a stretched position for one minute. For this reason, I subscribe to the progressive stretch routine. The routine is simple, come to a point of tension and hold for one minute. Then go deeper into the stretch by moving to the next point of tension, provided there is not any pain, and hold for another minute if possible. Continue to progress into a deeper stretch until you have completed three successive repetitions. Do not hold your breath while stretching. Breathing will help you release the muscle. Think of 'relaxing into the stretch'.

Note: These are general guidelines that Brett uses that have been effective in treating his patients. If the amount of time is too long or causing pain, please decrease the time to a tolerable level. If you start at 10 or 15 seconds that is okay, just don't give up. The more you devote yourself to stretching and overall conditioning, the larger the payoff will be.

Precaution: Do not push down on your body during a stretch to "push it further", you will feel the body letting go when it is ready. Relaxing and breathing into a stretch is very beneficial. Never push on a joint with your hands, place them on the supporting leg (the one not being stretched). Always work at your own level and progress at a rate that is comfortable for you.

SAMPLE STRETCH ROUTINE

Hamstring Stretch

There are four stretch exercises I subscribe to that are beneficial to those with posture problems. The first is the hamstring stretch. Start by sitting up on the edge of a chair with your back straight. If you are concerned that you might fall off the chair, please do this by the kitchen table so that you can hold on to something sturdy. Next, take your left leg forward and straighten your knee. Make sure your left heel is on the floor and your toes are pointing up toward the ceiling. At this point, you are ready to go into the stretch.

Place both hands above your right knee, then hinging (move torso forward) at your hip, lean forward keeping your chin up (level with the floor, eyes forward) until you feel slight tension in the back of the left thigh and knee. It is important to keep your back as straight as possible—do not worry how far you can go—that will increase the more limber you become. Remember, everyone has an individual stretch capacity. You may be more or less limber than average, don't worry about that. Just try your best. If you are stretching with a friend or family member, **never** push them into a stretch, this can cause serious damage.

Now you are ready to go into your progressive stretch. Hold for one minute if possible *(less time is okay, record how long you were able to stay in that position and try to increase it a little each time you perform the stretch)*, if tolerable, then lean a little further forward to the next point of tension and hold for another minute.

Repeat this cycle one more time for your third repetition. If you get to where you are fully stretched and there is no more moving to the next point of tension, just hold for the remainder of time in that one position, then switch and stretch the other leg.

Hip Flexor Stretch

The hip flexor stretch is performed while sitting in a chair for most people who are beginners to this stretch and have balance and/or knee issues. While sitting in a chair, rotate your body to the right so that your left leg is off the side. If possible, reach for the back of the chair. Hold this position for one minute (if possible), and then slide your left foot back to the next point of tension. If you are able to perform a forward pelvic tilt, you will feel this stretch even more.

Note: Do not perform this stretch if you are unstable on the chair or without supervision

Continue until you've completed three repetitions, bring yourself back centered on the chair, then rotate on the chair to your left so that your right leg is off the side. Repeat until you have completed three repetitions sliding your right foot back to the next point of tension.

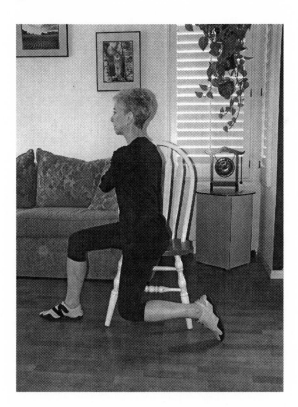

Corner Pec Stretch

The next stretch, the pectoralis (chest muscles) stretch, is performed standing in a corner with both hands on the wall about shoulder height (never above shoulder height), elbows in line with hands and with hands pointing slightly inward. With your feet arms length away from the corner, lean into the corner until you feel tension in your chest and shoulders. Hold this position (for up to a minute), then lean further into the corner if possible.

Again, it is important to note that one minute may be too long for some. Please adjust accordingly, but keep in mind research shows that stretching less than 30 seconds has little effect on lengthening muscles and other soft tissue. Nevertheless, if that is where you start, then that is okay, just remind yourself that you are succeeding and will get better.

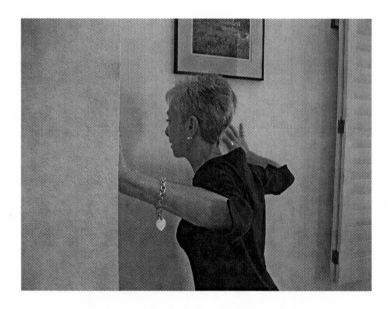

Concentrate on keeping your head up, chin tucked and level with the floor and back straight. We don't want your head to be hanging in front of your body as this places a big load on the muscles of your neck, nor do we want your low back to sway. **Pull your low belly muscles in towards your belly button to avoid low back stress in this position**.

Calf Stretch

This stretch involves you leaning into the wall. Place your hands on the wall with elbows slightly bent with right foot behind left, toes forward pointing at the wall. Slowly lean into the wall until you come to a point of tension, then hold for the prescribed amount of time. Then, lean into the next point of tension felt in your calf muscle.

After three repetitions, switch feet, placing the left leg behind the right. Concentrate on keeping your toe from turning outward, as this will decrease the amount of stretch on the calf muscle.

BEGINNING STRENGTH TRAINING ROUTINE

Strength plays a vital role in one's ability to balance. Without strength, it is exceptionally difficult to negotiate stairs, curbs, and transfer from chairs, recliners, cars, and other sitting surfaces. Moreover, muscular endurance or the ability to walk long distances without fatigue does rely on one's strength. The more strength and stamina and balance you possess, the less risk you have of falling.

GENERAL STRENGTH TRAINING PRINCIPLES

Before beginning this program, it is important to go over a few concepts that will bring you safety and optimal benefit. First, you always want to be under control when you perform these exercises, this means you keep your muscles active throughout the exercise. Allowing your muscles to relax while performing can cause serious injury. Likewise, posture plays a vital role in injury prevention during any exercise program.

Concentrate on keeping your head up, chin tucked (give yourself a double chin), chest lifted, and tummy tucked at all times. Think of pulling your belly button in toward the spine as if you were trying to tuck your shirt into some tight fitting slacks. This will provide the stability in your lower back that is needed to exercise safely. Finally, when pressing up against gravity, do not hold your breath as this will increase pressure against your heart. Instead, exhale slowly; inhale as you come back down.

Sit to Stand

The sit to stand exercise is one of the best to develop the extensor muscles of your lower body. These muscles are needed to walk with confidence. Sitting on the edge of the chair, place your feet under you and parallel (equal distance apart, facing forward), then with your hands positioned on the arms of the chair if needed, bring your nose over your toes, and push up to a standing position. Slowly return to the starting position by placing your hands on the arms of the chair and sitting back down. Repeat the exercise until you have completed the prescribed number of repetitions (usually 10-15, but the key is progression, start with the number of repetitions that you can safely complete using proper form).

Concentrate on using your legs more than arms. When you feel your legs are able to press you up without the use of your arms, progress to doing the exercise without your hands pressing off the arms of the chair, but always on your return slowly to sitting, make sure you find the arms of the chair with your hands for safety purposes.

Standing Hip Abduction

Begin this exercise by standing at the counter or behind a chair or walker. Hold onto the counter, chair or walker with your hands. Then, extend your right leg out to the side keeping both knees straight. Continue to extend the leg out then back next to the left leg until you have completed your repetitions. Then, switch to the left leg.

Standing vs. Walking Balance

Balance is broken down into two components; standing balance or walking (ambulatory) balance. The next sets of exercises have been designed to develop both components of balance. Your standing balance system is one that requires you to be able to balance without movement, while your walking balance system allows you to balance with movement.

STANDING BALANCE ROUTINE

This exercise program is considered a progressive program. This means, that in order to move to the next exercise, you need to have mastered the previous exercise. Each foot position will become increasingly harder. Likewise, in order be considering "mastering" a foot position, you must hold that position for 30 seconds on your first attempt.

Balance is much like a muscle, the more you exercise it, the stronger it will become. These exercises challenge your balance system so it is vital that you do these exercises in the presence of a caregiver or exercise professional. You should have a chair or walker placed in front of you and should have a caregiver or some-one who can be by your side or right behind you for safety. These exercises are extremely effective and within just a few sessions, you should see a marked improvement in your standing balance.

When you come to a position that you are not able to hold for thirty seconds retry three times. If, after the third try, you are unable to get a thirty second hold then write down the number of seconds that you were able to hold the position. Then, each session continue to record in the margin next to the exercise how long you are able to hold that position. With consistency, your time will increase. Invariably what will happen is you will see that you may not necessarily be able to hold it for thirty seconds but the number of seconds that you were able to hold will increase.

GUIDELINES FOR STANDING BALANCE ROUTINE

As with stretching and strengthening, it is important to establish general guidelines to follow when doing your static balance program.

1. Position yourself in a room 10 to 12 feet away from a wall with a walker or chair in front of you and a caregiver or other healthcare professional that is experienced in exercise programming behind you.

2. While holding onto the chair or walker, set your feet up in the position described in the exercise.

3. Look upward at a slight angle (not straight up to the ceiling) and when you feel you are balanced release your hold and bring your hands down by your side if possible. Continue to look upwards for 30 seconds while you balance in the prescribed foot position. These foot positions are very specific. It is important to pay careful attention to the position of the feet in the photos shown, as this will work to improve your balance. If you need to hold on to a sturdy piece of furniture for support that is okay, remember, progression is key, so stick with it!

4. Do not move to the next exercise until you are able to hold a progressive position with both feet for 30 seconds on your first attempt without losing your balance or needing to grab for chair/walker.

5. Don't give up. You can do this!

FEET SHOULDER WIDTH APART (Poor)

1. Stand with feet shoulder width apart as pictured while holding onto the walker or chair.

2. As soon as you feel comfortable, remove your hands from the walker or chair and hold for 30 seconds.

3. If, on your first attempt you are able to hold for 30 seconds without losing your balance, move on to the next exercise. If not, attempt two more times and record your best time.

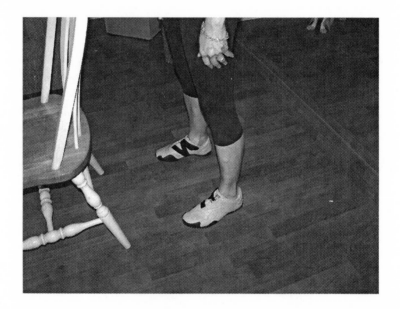

FEET SHOULDER WIDTH APART STAGGERED (Fair -)

1. Stand with feet shoulder width apart and staggered right foot in front of left as pictured while holding onto the walker or chair.

2. As soon as you feel comfortable, remove your hands from the walker or chair and hold for 30 seconds.

3. On your first attempt, if you are able to hold for 30 seconds without losing your balance, move on to the next exercise. If not, attempt two more times, record your best time, and then switch to Left foot in front of right.

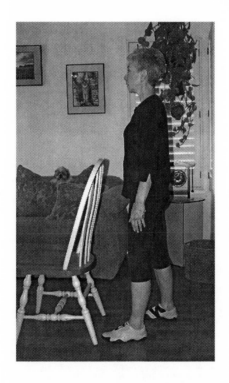

FEET TOGETHER (Fair)

1. Stand with feet together while holding the walker or chair.

2. As soon as you feel comfortable, remove your hands from the walker or chair and hold for 30 seconds.

3. If on your first attempt you are able to hold for 30 seconds without losing your balance, move on to the next exercise. If not, attempt two more times, and record your best time.

FEET TOGETHER STAGGERED 3" APART (Fair +)

1. Stand with big toe of your left foot 3 inches away from the heel of your right foot while holding onto your walker or chair.

2. As soon as you feel comfortable, remove your hands from the walker or chair and hold for 30 seconds.

3. If on your first attempt you are able to hold for 30 seconds without losing your balance, move on to the next exercise. If not, attempt two more times, record your best time, and then switch to Left foot in front of right.

FEET TOGETHER STAGGERED NO SEPARATION (Good -)

1. Stand with big toe of your left foot touching heel of your right foot while holding onto your walker or chair.

2. As soon as you feel comfortable, remove your hands from the walker or chair and hold for 30 seconds.

3. If on your first attempt you are able to hold for 30 seconds without losing your balance, move on to the next exercise. If not, attempt two more times, record your best time, then switch to Left foot in front of right.

FEET TOGETHER STAGGERED ONE FOOT BEHIND OTHER (Good)

1. Stand with big toe of your left STAGGERED and behind the heel of your right foot while holding onto your walker or chair.

2. As soon as you feel comfortable, remove your hands from the walker or chair and hold for 30 seconds.

3. If on your first attempt you are able to hold for 30 seconds without losing your balance, move on to the next exercise. If not, attempt two more times, record your best time, and then switch to Left foot in front of right.

FEET INLINE (Good +)

1. Stand with the big toe of your left behind the heel of your right foot while holding onto your walker or chair.

2. As soon as you feel comfortable, remove your hands from the walker or chair and hold for 30 seconds.

3. If on your first attempt you are able to hold for 30 seconds without losing your balance, move on to the next exercise. If not, attempt two more times, record your best time, then switch to left foot in front of right.

SINGLE LEG STANCE (Normal)

1. Stand on your right foot while holding onto your walker or chair.

2. As soon as you feel comfortable, remove your hands from the walker or chair and hold for 30 seconds.

3. If on your first attempt you are able to hold for 30 seconds, then switch to standing on your left foot for 30 seconds. If you are able to single leg stance on each foot for 30 seconds, congratulations, you have mastered your standing balance! If not, attempt two more times, record your best time, then switch to standing on your left foot.

THE WALKING BALANCE ROUTINE

The walking balance routine is very similar to the static program in that we are exercising the balance system by progressing from easy steps to more difficult. These types of steps are going to require you to walk or move along a hallway, preferably next to a rail.

> **RECOMMENDATION:** These exercises should be performed with the assistance of a caregiver or exercise professional for safety. Remember to consult your healthcare provider before beginning this or any exercise program.

Remember, we are challenging your balance system, which is the only way we can strengthen it. You will work to the edge of your balance ability each session. Likewise, your balance system needs to be conditioned and therefore this routine may likely take months to fully master. Please, do not be discouraged. Continue to perform the exercises daily, as they will improve your balance over time. As you work on increasing your balance, you will notice an increase in confidence and a decrease in fear of falling.

Finally, there are grades by each step. This grading will let you know where your balance is in relation to what is considered normal. Likewise, in order for you to be independent in your home without fear of falling, you need to have a grade of Good or better. Make this a goal if you live alone.

GUIDELINES FOR WALKING BALANCE ROUTINE

1.   Find an area that will allow you to walk for 20 feet. Have a caregiver near you for support and if possible perform these exercises next to a rail either on the deck or in a hallway.

2.   Keep your eyes focused on the ground 10 to 12 feet in front of you.

3.   While performing the step, attempt to maintain your balance without holding the rail or needing assistance from your caregiver.

4.   When you are able to perform the step without loss of balance or assistance from the rail or caregiver, progress to the next exercise. If you lose your balance, stop the routine! Record the distance you were able to step before losing your balance in the margin next to the exercise, then try to better that distance next workout.

     Do not progress to the next exercise until you have mastered the previous level. Balance being like a muscle, it would be foolish to ask you to lift a weight that is too heavy. Likewise, doing balance exercises that are too difficult, place you in a position to be seriously injured and will not help you improve your balance strength.

5.   Attempt to keep your steps continuous and symmetrical, with equal length, and little trunk sway.

6.   Don't give up. You can do this!

WALK FORWARD NO ASSISTANCE (Fair -)

Walk 20 feet without a walker or cane *(if you have been using any type of assistive device, do not attempt this exercise alone)* with feet shoulder width apart. Imagine a board between your legs and you have to keep your feet on each side of the board. If 20 feet is too much, start with five feet or less and practice daily to progress.

SIDE STEP (Fair)

Side step twenty feet in one direction, then side step twenty feet back. Stay facing the same way when you switch direction.

HIGH KNEE MARCH (Fair +)

Bring your knees up as high as you can as you march for twenty feet, turn around and march back for another twenty feet.

PLANK WALK (NARROW STANCE) (Good -)

The next exercise is called the "plank walk." Walk with your feet close together as if you are walking on a plank. It is important to take smaller steps but remember to come down on your heel first, try not to shuffle on flat feet.

BACKWARDS WALK (Good)

Walk backwards reversing the order of contact with your toe contacting the floor first then rolling off your heel.

CARRYOVER (Good)

As you side step cross over the front of your stance leg. Remain facing the same way each direction.

CARRYUNDER (Good)

As you side step, cross behind your stance leg. Remain facing the same way each direction.

LITTLE CROSSOVER (Good +)

Cross one foot over the other in one continuous motion. Do not allow the foot to make contact with the floor until it has passed over the other. Make sure there is a caregiver by your side and the rail on the other side in order to prevent any falls.

BRAIDING (CARRYOVER/UNDER) (Good +)

While side stepping cross over in front of your stance foot, then behind. Remain facing the same way up and back.

TANDEM WALK (WALK THE LINE) (Normal)

Bring your heel down right in front of your toe as if you were walking on a tight-rope. If you are able go twenty feet in both directions without any assistance or help, congratulations you have normal walking balance!

WALKING ENDURANCE PROGRAM

Finally, it is important as you develop your endurance as well. This is best done by distance walking. Four-wheel walkers with built in seats are perfect for this program in that they allow you to sit down whenever you get tired. Go for a walk everyday and try to go a little bit further each time—progression is key. Challenge yourself to take a few more steps every day. Attempt to keep steps continuous and symmetrical, with equal length, and little trunk sway as the quality of your steps are just as important as the number of them taken.

YOU CAN DO THIS!

One of my patients, age 86, underwent her fourth hip replacement (two on each side). She was an avid golfer who had to given up play due to her hip problems. Understandably, she became depressed as she saw the quality of her life slip away. For six months, she went from Bedroom to Recliner to Bedroom, day in and day out. Finally, I was called to work with her. She was weak, and unable to stand without someone's assistance. Moreover, her walking balance was extremely poor, as she needed a walker and assistance to get from room to room in her home.

We began working with her strength and range of motion on the bed. Once her strength levels were adequate, we began working on her standing balance, and then her walking balance. Slowly, over time, she began to improve. After six months of doing the very same exercises, I have taught you in this book, she was able to walk without a walker or cane independently.

It was now time to work on her golf game. First, we went to the putting green at the local club. Then she progressed to chipping, then pitching, and finally ½ to ¾ swings on the range. By now a year had passed. She was 87 and ready to play golf once again. I will never forget the look in her eye when she tee'd up her first ball to play for the first time in two years. It was priceless.

You can also overcome your injury or illness. Sure, it will take work, and it will take time. You have always been a fighter; you would not have picked up this book or lived this long if you weren't. With just a few exercises a day, and determination to get back to the life you once had, you can improve your balance and your life. You can do this!

One day, you too may be teeing up your ball on the first hole, or dining out with family. Maybe you will find evening walks with the one you love enjoyable once again. You can do this!

Progression and More

Author: Joanne Price

Once you have worked on balance, increasing strength and stretching, building your muscles will become your next goal. Consider joining an exercise class or gym. If you go consistently, the payoff is well worth the monthly dues. People who exercise regularly enjoy a higher quality of life. With regular exercise, you will notice an increase in energy, vitality and maybe make a few new friends along the way.

There is, however, one muscle that you probably want to work in the privacy of your own home. Working on the toning of this particular muscle will help keep you from 'rushing' to the bathroom, thereby lowering your risk of falling. The particular exercise I speak of is called a Kegal exercise. The muscles in the pubic area also need a good workout so they can help you control the flow and urgency of urination. This exercise is easily performed (and no one needs to know when you are doing it!).

KEGAL EXERCISES

Begin by sitting upright in a chair, holding your best posture! Pull up and in on the pubic muscles (visualize stopping the flow of urine). Then hold for a few seconds, you will notice your low belly has pulled up and in (a great side benefit!). If you practice this exercise a few times a day for several repetitions each time, you will begin to notice that you do not need to rush to the bathroom.

You will be able to hold the contraction for longer periods the more you practice, initially you might only be able to hold the contraction for a moment or two—as most of us have not ever worked this muscle, which is why you need to! Eventually, you will be able to 'hold it' until you are ready, thus lowering your risk of falling by not needing to rush to the bathroom. For more information about Kegal exercises, ask your Urologist or primary care doctor.

FOOT EXERCISES

Inappropriate footwear and lack of circulation can cause a decrease in your ability to balance. In order to even begin to facilitate increasing balance, stability and endurance, you should to pay attention to your feet. Have you ever seen someone who was born with out the use of his or her arms or was born with no arms? You may have noticed how they were able to use their feet to grab and hold things with their toes and feet. Or, look at a baby's feet, they can open their toes wide and use them to grab items as well. Since the time you were less than a year old, your feet have been 'stuffed' into containers and barely allowed any freedom. Your feet work hard for you every day—pay them a little attention and maybe they will be able to contribute to an increase in your balance.

RECOMMENDATIONS:

- Try spelling the alphabet with your feet. Take off your shoes and write in the air letters A—L on one side then switch to M-Z on the other. Then try opening your toes, at first, you may not be able to but with good old-fashioned determination and a little diligence, you can do this! Try this each day.

- When getting out of bed, before you feet touch the floor, point and flex the feet a few times and scrunch and open the toes. This will help get circulation to the area before applying weight. Think of it as waking up your feet before asking them to work for you.

- Visit a podiatrist regularly to check on the health of your feet. Pay particular attention if you have circulatory issues or diabetes.

- Keep your feet well groomed.

ADAPTATIONS FOR SUCCESS

Even if you have a very healthy lifestyle, and you've 'done everything right', health issues can arise due to genetics or unfortunate circumstances, such as a bad accident, that create an increase if your personal risk of falling. Some of us are confronted with grip issues. Whether due to arthritis or some other malady, holding on to weights for purposes of strength training may not be an option. Grip issues can be easily worked with and should not be allowed to get in the way of building strength. Weights now come in multiple configurations other than the old-fashioned dumbbell style. There are weighted balls, flat weights, and many types of resistance bands that can be utilized for working on building muscle strength.

Remember; where there is a will, there is a way! Motivation is the key to success. For strength training, you can use your own body weight, as in wall push-ups or the exercise, 'Sit and Stand'. Strength can not rebuild itself; you must work on it daily. The exercise industry had made great strides in the area of 'senior' exercise. Take advantage of the knowledge out there and the new equipment that the ever-evolving exercise industry has come up with to help you achieve your goals.

Mind-Body Connection

As we all know, stress takes a toll on our bodies over time. Sometimes stress is a significant component in the onset of certain chronic medical conditions. Stress can also increase your risk of falling, as some of the symptoms of too much stress can be quite distracting. If we are under a high degree of stress, we are unable to relax.

Stress affects our physical and emotional wellbeing. Consequently, I have decided to include stress reduction as a strategy to reduce fall risk because I have seen, first hand, the effects of the techniques discussed here. When practiced consistently, you may notice not only a feeling of calm awareness, but also increased clarity of thought, energy and an over all increase in positive thoughts. Recognizing the mind-body connection may help in reducing your risk of falling and sustaining serious injury.

BREATHING

Thinking back, I do not think I actually knew how to breathe properly until I was about 35. That is when I took my first yoga class. I breathed so deeply (per the instruction of the teacher) that I became dizzy the first time. It was only after a few classes that I realized that I had not been really breathing fully, but rather (and this is the case for many of us) taking short small breaths, barely feeding my body and brain the oxygen it needed to survive!

Breath is vital to support all bodily functions. Moreover, most of us don't do it enough. Why? Well, my belief is that between stress, hectic lifestyles and not paying attention to our breathing we lose our natural pattern of breath and take on short, shallow breathing. Increasing oxygen levels is something we can all do, it is easy and all it requires is an awareness of how to breathe correctly.

There are many types of 'breathing' programs available for you to try. The one that I have personally used and taught some principles from in my exercises classes is the program developed by Dr. Andrew Weil, called *'Breathing'*. It comes in various forms, the one I learned from came on a two CD set. It begins with a discussion of the value of breath and then goes into specific breathing exercises that will help you increase the oxygen levels to your body and brain and help relieve stress. Look for it in your local library or bookstore. There are many other programs available, chose what works for you. Again, I recommend checking at your local library as a first resource.

VISUALIZATION

Have you ever heard anyone say, "If you can see it, you can do it?" Visualization, combined with breath techniques have been shown to help athletes perform better, acrobatic pilots fly their routines more precisely, pregnant moms give birth without pain medication, and it can help you reduce your risk of falling.

If you visualize yourself falling safely and then getting up successfully from a fall, you may be more likely to 'fall the right way' if it happens to you. I urge to you read the section in the book on how to fall properly and then visualize yourself doing just that and surviving, unhurt. By 'seeing' yourself survive safely, you may not panic if you do fall. Panicking during a fall works against you in that panic raises stress levels, which, in turn, will exacerbate certain medical condition symptoms.

For general stress reduction, visualize any thoughts that bring peace to your soul. Whether relaxing on beautiful vista watching a sunset over the water, or floating in a boat along a lazy river, create a journey that is stress free and enjoyable in your minds eye and you will feel the difference. There are audio tapes and CD's available that can teach you visualization relaxation techniques. Check your local library or bookstore for more information.

APPENDIX

RECORD YOUR FALLS

Date: _____ Time of Day: _____

Location of Fall: _____

How did you fall (ex: Tripping, Lost Balance): _____

_____

Circumstances (What were you doing at the time of the accident?)

_____

_____

Prior to the incident, what were you doing?

_____

_____

_____

_____

What can you change or do differently to decrease your risk of this type of fall?

_____

_____

_____

By documenting the details of a fall as soon as possible afterwards, you may be able to identify a relationship between a 'type' of fall and the circumstances surrounding the accident. With this knowledge, you have the opportunity to address and implement the necessary changes that may lower or eliminate the risk, which contributed to the 'type' of fall, you experienced. Use this form to begin a dialog with your healthcare provider and family members on ways they may assist you in the reduction of your risk of falling.

MEDICATION REVIEW FORM TEMPLATE

This form is an example of what you may use to list your medications and supplements for review by your healthcare provider and pharmacist. Request a drug interaction review periodically. This template has been filled in with sample information to show an example for you in filling out your own information. Include OTC medications and supplements on your actual review sheet. If writing is not feasible, you can use the 'brown bag method'. Place your pill containers in a sack and bring them in for review. This method usually requires a special appointment. You can drop off a list of your medications for a review and pick up the information later.

Name: <u>John Patient</u> Date: <u>   January 10, 2006   </u>

Contact Number: <u>   555-122-3456   </u>

1—Medication Name/Strength: <u>Digoxin, 35 mg per tablet</u> Duration: <u>Ongoing</u>

Dosage: <u>   1 tablet twice a day with meals   </u>

Prescribing Physician: <u>   Dr. Virginia Bailey   </u> Ph #: <u> 555-432-1234   </u>

Patient Concerns: <u>   Nausea, Dizziness, Not Hungry   </u>

2—Medication Name/Strength: <u>Baby Aspirin, 10 mg per tablet</u> Duration: <u> Ongoing</u>

Dosage: <u> 1 pill day with meals   </u>

Prescribing Physician: <u>   NA   </u> Ph #: <u>   </u>

Patient Concerns: <u>Not sure if I need to take this, recommended by a friend</u>

3—Medication Name/Strength: <u>   </u> Duration: <u>   </u>

Dosage: <u>   </u>

Prescribing Physician: <u>   </u> Ph #: <u>   </u>

Patient Concerns: _____

5—Medication Name/Strength: _____ Duration: _____

Dosage: _____

Prescribing Physician: _____ Ph #: _____

Patient Concerns: _____

HOME SAFETY, FALL RISK REDUCTION CHECKLIST

Use this list checklist as a guideline to assess each room for fall safety and possible home modification requirements. Each home is different, so this checklist may not address your particular needs. Guidelines for home safety universally include lack of clutter and a simplified floor plan. Home safety modifications should be prepared for and completed before a fall occurs—being proactive is a key to success in this area. The older we get, the harder adapting to change can become. Check off each item from your list as it is completed.

Bathroom

- Adequate lighting, as we age we need more light to see clearly (60 watt bulbs)
- Nightlights, lighted path to bathroom
- Flashlight (recommend trying a tap light for ease of use) on night-stand
- Grab Bars (toilet, bath, around sink)
- High rise toilet seat with dual arm support (verify integrity of seat regularly)
- Non-skid mat or other gripping material on shower floor
- Secure sink and counter
- Adequate and centralized storage for oils/lotions
- Eliminate clutter
- Shower seat or transfer bench if needed
- Change from liquid soap to 'soap on a rope' or a mounted soap/shampoo container
- Removable shower head with hose and long handle
- Adaptive devices—there are may options for getting into and out of the shower, see your medical supply store representative for more information or options

Kitchen

- Adequate lighting
- All items can be reached without needing stepstool
- Grab handles near counters
- Level flooring, no cracks or nicks
- Floor risers (thresholds) less than ¼ inch and secure
- Eliminate slip hazards such as area rugs
- Eliminate clutter
- Sturdy kitchen table/chairs
- Open pathways

Halls/Stairways

- Adequate Lighting
- Light switches—top and bottom
- Reflective tape/paint on stairs
- Level stairs
- Sturdy and secure handrail
- Steps of uniform width and height
- No items left on stairs
- Install a ramp with handrail or automated chair to get up and down stairs

Bedroom

- Adequate lighting
- Sturdy nightstand
- Tap lights, flashlight operational and within reach from bed
- Lighted path to bathroom
- Bedside rail and or grab bars
- Bedclothes that do not bunch or hang on to floor
- Clear pathway to bathroom

- Eliminate closet clutter and excess furniture
- Needed items within reach from bedside

Furniture/Floors

- Sturdy, adequate height
- Firm chairs and sofas (no sinking)
- Clear pathways—36" to 42"
- Eliminate any wires or cords in pathways (secure along wall edges)
- Remove glass furniture
- Eliminate floor clutter
- Remove slip hazards (area rugs)
- Check for loose carpet tacks
- Carpeting secure
- Eliminate long pile carpeting, opt for short pile

General

- Wear proper footwear
- Avoid flowing clothing/robes
- Current eyewear prescription (take extra care if wearing progressive lenses)
- Current medical info posted in kitchen and on person when out
- **Emergency Response System installed and in use**
- Lockbox installed for access by emergency medical personnel
- Neighbor key or lockbox code
- Outside stairs safe/sturdy, install railings where needed
- Appropriate eyewear (prescription sunglasses if needed for outside)
- Have a telephone you can reach from the floor
- Level outside walkways
- Functional smoke detectors
- Mark outside curbs and steps with paint

- Carry a whistle or cellular phone (or both) during excursions
- Have walkers/canes checked regularly for wear and tear
- Have walkers/canes checked for proper alignment for your height
- Carry medication list and emergency contact information on your person
- Wear Hip Protectors

How to Fall

A fall can happen anytime, even if you do everything right including diet, exercise, medication management and home modifications. A fall can occur just by walking in a straight line, down the hallway, in the middle of the day. There are two kinds of falls. Falls you can do something about (like better posture, diet and home modifications), and falls you can't (leg muscles give out). As we all know, knowledge is power—it is best to learn how to fall properly and how to get up from a fall, if possible.

For your practice, visualize the process of falling correctly and rising unharmed. Below are suggestions adapted by those from the Academy of Orthopedic Surgeons. We are not suggesting to practice falling, just visualizing a safe fall and easy recovery. This may help reduce fear and increase your confidence, helping to reduce your risk of a fall.

1. **RELAX.** Tense muscles will transmit the shock of the fall to the less protected parts of the body. You may be able to aim your fall if you do not panic, thus avoiding hazardous edges.

2. **DO NOT REACH.** Using your hands to 'break' your fall can result in sprains, dislocations, or breaks of the fingers, wrists, arms, or shoulders.

3. **PROTECT YOUR HEAD**. Tuck your chin, and try to bring both hands to your head. This will not only protect your head, it will keep you from reaching out to break your fall.

4. **BEND YOUR KNEES.** Try to bend your knees and squat as much as possible. This will bring you closer to the ground, thus reducing the force of the impact. Think of tuck and roll.

5. **AVOID BONY SURFACES.** Avoid letting any part of the body where the bone is close to the skin strike hard surfaces. This includes hips, knees, ankles, heels, elbows, spine, and head.

6. **SPREAD THE SHOCK.** Spread the force of impact evenly over the entire body on soft surfaces such as the buttocks, forearms, thighs, and calves.

7. **BREATHE.** Remain calm by taking full breaths.

How to Get Up After a Fall

If you have a medic alert pendant, press the button to summon help. ***If you think you have a serious injury, do not get up***. Instead, activate your medical alert device or call 911 (remember to always have a phone within reach from the floor). After a fall, assess your body. Wiggle fingers and toes, relaxing the body for several minutes if necessary. Take several slow full breaths and remind yourself to feel confident that you are okay, and you can get up. If you do feel strong enough to get up, the following steps are a guideline. Remember, each situation is different. It some cases it is safest to not move at all.

Relax, and assess your situation. If you are in pain, stay where you are and call for help. If you have a medical alert button—press it and request help from the operator. They will call help for you. If you want to try to get up:

1. Turn your head in the direction of the roll. Roll over onto the side of your body that hurts the least.

2. Pull your legs into the fetal position, and place the hand that is on the upward arm in front of your chest.

3. Using the hand in front of the chest, press yourself upward into a sitting position.

4. If you can, crawl to a strong, stable piece of furniture like a couch or chair. Approach from the front and put both hands on the seat.

5. Slowly, begin to rise. Bend whichever knee is stronger, and keep your other knee on the floor. Push down with your arms to lift yourself.

6. Slowly rotate your torso around and sit on the chair or couch.

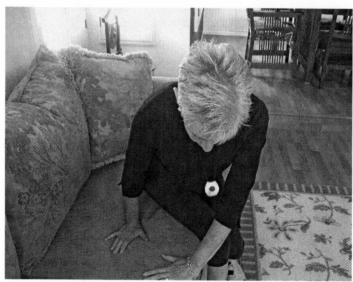

Closing

No book can be everything to everybody. However, it is the goal of all who contributed to this book to provide our readers with a practical, easy to implement plan that will help you and remain independent and safe for as long as possible. Please share this book with your friends and family. If we all pitch in, we can make a positive difference for ourselves and those we love. What applies to your particular situation may not be applicable for someone else. It is important for you to be pro-active and take the necessary steps that will lower fall risk in your particular situation.

The difference between knowing and doing is **MOTIVATION**! You now have learned different strategies to lower your fall risk. We hope you feel motivated to take the steps necessary carry through with what you have learned from this guide.

As Winston Churchill once said, "Never Give Up, Never Give Up.... Never, Ever Give Up!"

References

Hansdorff J.M. Rios, DA and Edelbar, H.K. (2001). **Gait variability a fall risk in community living older adults: A 1 year prospective study**. Archives of Physical medicine and Rehabilitation, 2, 1050–1056.

Shaughnessy, AF.**Common Drug Interactions in the Elderly**, Emergency Medicine 24(21):21, 1992

Archstone Foundation, **Preventing Falls in Older Californians: State of the Art**, Long Beach, CA, January 2003, revised October 2004

Archives of the American Academy of Orthopaedic Surgeons, **Falls and the Elderly**, Vol 2, No. 1, Winter 1998

Tinetti, Mary E., Williams, Christianna S., **Falls, Injuries Due to Falls, and the Risk of Admission to a Nursing Home**, N Engl J Med 1997 337: 1279–1284

Thapa, Purushottam B., Gideon, Patricia, Cost, Terry W., Milam, Amanda B., Ray, Wayne A., **Antidepressants and the Risk of Falls among Nursing Home Residents**, N Engl J Med 1998 339: 875-882

The AGS Foundation for Health in Aging, **A Patients Guide to Preventing Falls**, Pamphlet, www.healthinaging.org

HomeWatch LLC, **F.I.P.'s Program Fall Injury Prevention, A Collaborative Program**, 2003

Bischoff-Ferrari, B. Dawson-Hughes, WC. Willett, et al., **Effect of vitamin D on falls.** HA. JAMA, 2004, vol.291, pp. 1999–2006

Emergency Medical Services, AIS, San Diego County, **Elderly Falls Report**, Aug. 2005

Nickolaus, T, Bach M. **Preventing falls in community-dwelling frail older people using a home intervention team (HIT): results from the randomized falls HIT trial.** J Am Geriatric Soc March 2003

Agostini, Joseph v., Doreothy I.Baker and Sydney T. Bogardus, **Making Health Care Safer: A Critical Analysis of Patient Safety Practices.** The Agency for Healthcare Research and Quality, July 2001

Gregg EW, Pereira MA, Caspersen, CJ. **Physical activity, falls and fractures among older adults: a review of the epidemiologic evidence"** Journal of the American Geriatric Society, Aug 2000

Kannus, Pekka, Jari Parkkari, et al. **Prevention of Hip fracture in Elderly People with the use of a Hip Protector.** N Engl J Med., Nov 2000

Lui, BA., AD Topper, et al. **Falls among older people: Relationship to medication use and hypotension.** Journal of American Geriatric Society, 1995.

About The Authors

Joanne Price, CEO, Integricare Corporation

Joanne Price is the CEO of Integricare Corporation. The mission of Integricare is to help older adults lead independent and safe lives through offering supportive services and education. Integricare is the umbrella organization of ResponseLink of San Diego County (www.responselinksd.com), a medical alarm distributorship operated by Joanne and her husband Marc. Joanne is an active member of several industry groups including the San Diego Council on Aging and the San Diego Regional Home Care Council. Her philanthropic affiliations include being a member of the speaker's bureau for the San Diego and Imperial County Alzheimer's Association, the San Diego Chapter of the Arthritis Foundation, and San Diego County Aging and Independence Services, which she is past chairperson of the Fall Prevention Task Force. As an experienced exercise instructor, she substitute teaches for the *Feeling Fit Club*, a county sponsored community based exercise program for older adults.

Joanne is a popular speaker and educator on the topics of fall prevention and healthy aging, providing informative and motivating presentations to older adults and care provider groups in her community including the Parkinson's Disease Association of San Diego, local chapters of AARP and numerous support and professional groups. She has produced and directed her own televised exercise series, *Stairway to Fitness* (2002–03) and has held numerous fitness certifications. Early in 2006 she co-produced a fall prevention video, 'Don't Fall for It!' for residents of San Diego county through grant funds provided from both the department of Aging and Independence Services and Scripps Mercy Hospital and Trauma Center San Diego. In 2005 she co-authored an online CEU Fall Prevention course for healthcare workers through Caretrain, Inc. which can be found at www.caretrain.com. She also provides CEU training for Social Workers and Geriatric Case Managers.

Please address book comments or presentation inquiries to Ms. Price through her web site at www.fallpreventioninfo.com.

Patricia-Jo Dean, RN

A registered nurse for over 30 years, Patricia is an experienced clinical and administrative nurse with an extensive acute and long term care background. She has worked as Director of Nursing in several facilities in her area and is sought after for both her administrative style and her hands on, caring approach to patient care. For many years Patricia has been a strong advocate for patients and families. She is an active participant in facility committees, such as Admission Committee, CQI, Safety Committee, and Chairperson of Falls and Restraint Reduction Committee. She has developed educational programs for nursing personnel for Skilled Nursing Facilities in Massachusetts. In early 2005, Patricia co-authored a CEU Fall Prevention course for healthcare workers through Caretrain, Inc. which can be found at www.caretrain.com. Patricia received her certification as a Gerontological Nurse in the quest for continuing her knowledge in the field of healthcare for older adults.

Brett Longo, Physical Therapist

Brett Longo is a Physical Therapist who has devoted the last eight years of his career to working with elderly people in the home health setting. He now works for More Than Physical Therapy Health Services located in the San Diego County as the Director of Community Education. Brett has extensive training in balance re-education for those advancing in age, and feels this is a very important aspect to maintaining quality of life for older adults.

Amy McAllister, Registered Dietitian

As an ADA registered dietitian, living and working in Rhode Island. Amy has developed nutritional programs for several retirement communities. As a nutritional educator, Amy works to help patients create practical nutritional programs to better control their individual medical conditions. Her areas of focus include cardiac rehabilitation, weight loss and diabetes. As contributor for the online course and this text, Amy seeks to assist people in furthering their knowledge of the importance of proper nutrition and hydration for maximum well-being. Amy co-authored a CEU Fall Prevention course for healthcare workers through Caretrain, Inc. which can be found at www.caretrain.com.

978-0-595-42016-2
0-595-42016-8